Wrestling with Singleness

Wrestling

with

Singleness

FINDING STRENGTH IN GOD TO LIVE IT WELL

Megan Lyon

Wrestling with Singleness

Copyright © 2018 by Megan Lyon

"Make Pure," in *Rose from Brier* by Amy Carmichael, © 1933 by The Dohnavur Fellowship. Used by permission of CLC Publications. May not be further reproduced. All rights reserved.

THE SILVER CHAIR by C.S. Lewis copyright © C.S. Lewis Pte. Ltd. 1953. Extract reprinted by permission.

THE GREAT DIVORCE by C.S. Lewis copyright © C.S. Lewis Pte. Ltd. 1946. Extract reprinted by permission.

Song: Psalm 46 (Lord of Hosts) Written by: Jennie Lee Riddle/Josiah Warneking/Josh Miller/Shane Barnard. Copyright: © 2015 Jennie Lee Riddle Music (BMI) (div. of New Nation Music) / Tent Peg Music(BMI) (div. of New Nation Music) (both admin. by Music Services) / Songs From Wellhouse (BMI) (admin. by Wellhouse Entertainment LLC) All Rights Reserved.

Cover Design: Bekah Tuttle

First printing 2018

Printed in the United States of America

All Scripture quotations, unless otherwise indicated, are taken from the Holy Bible, New International Version®, NIV®. Copyright ©1973, 1978, 1984, 2011 by Biblica, Inc.™ Used by permission of Zondervan. All rights reserved worldwide. www.zondervan.com The "NIV" and "New International Version" are trademarks registered in the United States Patent and Trademark Office by Biblica, Inc.™

Scripture quotations marked NLT are taken from the Holy Bible, New Living Translation, copyright ©1996, 2004, 2007, 2013, 2015 by Tyndale House Foundation. Used by permission of Tyndale House Publishers, Inc., Carol Stream, Illinois 60188. All rights reserved.

Scripture quotations marked NASB are taken from the New American Standard Bible® (NASB), Copyright © 1960, 1962, 1963, 1968, 1971, 1972, 1973, 1975, 1977, 1995 by The Lockman Foundation Used by permission. www.Lockman.org.

All emphases in Scripture quotations have been added by the author.

ISBN: 978-0-9998794-0-5 (paperback)
ISBN: 978-0-9998794-1-2 (ePub)

God is the strength of my heart and my portion forever.
Psalm 73:26

Dedicated to all the single ladies
who are wrestling with the tension
of life not turning out the way they dreamed.

Contents

INTRODUCTION

The idea that our dreams might not come true can fill us with dread. The longer we have had these dreams, the tighter we cling to them. Few dreams are as universal as the one for marriage.

As little girls, most of us imagined weddings. Ken married Barbie countless times. We pretended to get married by dressing up as a bride and forcing our friends or sisters to stand in as the groom. Maybe you were the younger sister forced to be the groom, dreaming of your turn to be the bride.

We had our favorite Disney princesses. Certainly, someday our prince would come for us. That was always the plan. That was always the dream. As young adults, most of us have planned our weddings in our heads multiple times. Many of us have a private Pinterest board where we have assembled a compilation of what we hope our dream wedding will someday look like in real life. Waking up every day in a bed by ourselves, though, is a constant reminder that our dream has not come true.

From what I have experienced in my life and seen in the lives of those around me, there comes a moment—or several moments—in our mid-to-late twenties where we start thinking for the first time that maybe our "someday" will never come.

What if marriage is not what the Lord has *for me*?

I began to consider this possibility after my college graduation. I had recently moved into my first adult apartment with three friends from college. I do not remember what prompted my sudden realization; maybe it was because I was twenty-three with no romantic prospects. But I distinctly remember standing in that apartment thinking about how I had been single for the past five years. I then realized the *next* five years could pass by exactly the same as the previous five, and in five years I could still be single. *Gasp, oh the horror!* I laugh now as I write this and look back on that moment. While I had hoped I would be wrong, it has since proven to be true.

We are often okay with singleness for a season, but the majority of us would like to get married. Most of us are not running around volunteering as tribute to be single forever. I have expanded my original thought as I have realized that the next five years, and the next five, and the next five could all pass by the same way. I could find myself in my forties and single. And I may go through my entire life never having been married.

It is funny how sometimes life does not work out the way you thought it would. For several years I have volunteered as a youth leader in my church's teen ministry. One night we played an icebreaker game where each person partnered up with someone for a question-answer segment. The leader shouted out a question and you told your partner the answer. The questions were random and you switched partners for every question.

One time the leader shouted, "How old do you want to be when you get married?"

With a smirk, I told my partner (a teenage girl), "Twenty-three!"

She had a look of confusion on her face when she asked,

"Wait, how old are you?"

I replied with a half-smile, "Twenty-six."

She laughed a little and said, "I thought you were older than twenty-three."

Sorry kid, life doesn't always turn out the way you dream, plan, hope, or pray.

Somewhere along the line, most girls tend to formulate an age at which they would like to get married. They are fine getting married before then, but they would at least like to have a husband by that age. For me, it was twenty-three. For my one of my best friends, it was twenty-eight. When that year came and went, though, it was rough.

Many who know me would tell me they do not think I should give up on the possibility that someday I will get married. I would like to hold out hope that someday a man would ask me to marry him. But no one may come for me, other than the Lord Himself. In reality, I could be single for the rest of my life. I have had several moments of alarm, panic, and distress over the years as I have realized that this might not be a temporary phase that I need to endure.

When I was in college there were almost no single women in their thirties in my church. Every year I have seen this number increase and now I am one of them. As I approached my thirtieth birthday I thought it would be good for me to write out the top ten lessons I have learned in singleness. I kept putting it off, not really wanting to think about all of this. At the beginning of 2017, I forced myself to write it out. Afterward, I thought I could write a book on this.

Nothing has surprised me more than how encouraging writing and reviewing these thoughts has been to my own heart. I hope that you find this book encouraging to your own heart as well.

As I have talked with other single women, I have recognized how much of a commonality there is between us all. Life can be hard. Singleness can be hard. There can be days where trying to hold onto truth feels like trying to hold onto sand. Some days our emotions are a hot mess as we wrestle with desires, fears, and doubts. Often we find ourselves going over the same questions again and again. As we process through these questions, there are key truths we need to remember. Some of my thoughts are not specific to singleness and are applicable to trials in general. However, I wrestle with these thoughts the most in relation to being single.

If I am going to be single, I want to live it well for God. Whether I am single or married, I do not want to waste the life the Lord has given me. Deciding that I want to live it well does not automatically make it easy. More than I fear perpetual singleness, however, I fear wasting the rest of my life worrying about if I am going to get married.

I want us to live our single lives in a way that honors and pleases the Lord. Living that way requires us to remember what is true and to not get lost in discouragement and doubt.

This world needs believers to be a light in the darkness. This is no less true in any season of life, but it is especially needed when it comes to being single and living for the Lord. I believe we can be that light. We can be single and live it well.

ONE

* * * * * *

WHERE IS HOPE FOUND?

*As for us, from morning until lights-out,
whenever we were not in ranks for roll
call, our Bible was the center of an
ever-widening circle of help and hope. . .
The blacker the night around us grew,
the brighter and truer and more beautiful
burned the word of God.*

Corrie ten Boom, *The Hiding Place*

Facing unfulfilled desires is uncomfortable and painful. Many people try to avoid facing them as much as possible. It would be easier if everything turned out the way we wanted.

Our own hearts often cause us to put our hope in the wrong thing. We tend to put too much hope in seeing all our desires and dreams fulfilled.

After college, I was living in that apartment with three friends, and we found ourselves in a dilemma. It took a few weeks to surface because none of us spent that much time cooking. When we did cook, it became obvious. Even though we pooled our kitchen supplies, we had some serious gaps.

The largest gap was in the pots and pans category, or I should say the pot category. We had one pot. If you wanted to cook pasta, you could not boil noodles and make sauce at the same time. There were other gaps, but this one still sticks out in my mind years later.

The entire blame did not rest on my roommates. My personal inventory of kitchen items when I moved in was two bowls, two mugs, and a toaster. If I was going to transition to the adult world, this was not going to cut it for very long. But the lack of essential cooking gear did not bother any of us enough to try to remedy the situation quickly.

After a few months, I began to question why I was so hesitant to buy additional kitchen items. Being a recent college graduate, I had plenty of student loan debt, but money did not seem to be stopping me. Eventually, I realized my greatest source of reluctance: I did not want to buy things I would soon be putting on a wedding registry.

I continued to hold out hope that marriage was right around the corner, even though I was not dating anyone. At twenty-three, I was banking on getting married soon, and I did not need to buy any more items for the kitchen. When we are unwilling to do something that is not sin, we should check our underlying motivations. My heart was set on my desire to get married soon. Once reality settled in that I had no real reason to think I was getting married soon, I bought some more pots.

If you are not in a serious romantic relationship, you should not be counting on getting married soon. Putting our hope in marriage can look different for each of us. I was putting my hope in marriage by counting on the wedding registry for kitchen items. Others of us might delay buying a house; because it is something we pictured doing with a husband. We are reluctant to go on vacation somewhere because we imagined we would go there on a honeymoon.

It is hard not to put hope in something you think is certainly coming your way. If you think marriage is coming your way, it is hard not to get your hope, your heart, and your joy all wrapped up in the prospect of it. The longer you remain single, the heavier your heart feels. For a woman who wants to be married, life can feel bleak when there is no prospect of getting married anytime soon.

When life feels bleak, little red flags should rise in your mind. You need to consider: Are you putting too much hope in temporary circumstances? I know my heart should be less wrapped up in fleeting pleasures, but it is hard when they are tangible.

Hope is a funny thing to try to wrap my mind around. The only way to measure if it is placed in the right thing is when circumstances seem to be stacked against me. When things are not going my way, I see more clearly what I am putting my hope in based on the reaction in my heart. If I overreact, it shows my focus is on the wrong thing.

We tend to rely on tangible things, more than on God. Leaning on tangible things, more than on God creates false hope. It can be tempting to think we will achieve a greater sense of security and fulfillment when we get married. Hoping in something other than God for these things, however, will always prove unreliable regardless of your relationship status.

Job's friend said something similar: "'So perishes the hope of the godless. What they trust in is fragile; what they rely on is a spider's web. They lean on the web, but it gives way; they cling to it, but it does not hold'" (Job 8:13–15). When our hope is not in the Lord, eventually we realize that what we are leaning on is only as solid as a spider's web.

HOPE IN THE LORD

The more our hope is in the temporary, the more we will feel disappointed by things in this life. If my hope is in the Lord, then it will not feel like the world is crashing down around me. It will not seem as if there is no light at the end of the tunnel.

This does not mean we will have no heartache, pain, or grief. We will experience these when life does not turn out the way we planned. We should grieve our losses, but let us not grieve as the world that has no hope (1 Thess. 4:13). No matter how dire the circumstances, there is always hope with the Lord.

Countless times the Bible encourages us to put our hope in God more than anything else. "Israel, put your hope in the Lord both now and forevermore" (Ps. 131:3). It is hard sometimes for me to grasp what "having my hope in the Lord" even means. I have come to see that it primarily means two things: (1) believing and trusting in the Lord's character, and (2) looking forward to spending an eternity in heaven with Him.

Throughout the Old Testament, the writers point to who the Lord is as their source of hope. Lamentations is a great example of the writer's hope in the midst of distress. "He has besieged and surrounded me with anguish and distress" (Lam. 3:5 NLT). Jeremiah's trials caused him to be in emotional distress and despair. But in that anguish, he looks to the Lord as his source of hope.

> Yet I still dare to hope when I remember this: The faithful love of the Lord never ends! His mercies never cease. Great is his

faithfulness; his mercies begin afresh each morning. I say to myself, "The Lord is my inheritance; therefore, I will hope in him!" (Lam. 3:21-24 NLT)

The reason Jeremiah dared to hope was because of his firm belief in the Lord's character. He reminded himself of the Lord's love, mercy, and faithfulness and clung to the truth of those things. No matter how grim our circumstances, we can always look to the Lord. Regularly reading the Bible helps us to remember the Lord's character and nature.

Our confidence should be in the Lord more than in anyone else. The Lord alone can promise and perfectly keep His word, "Never will I leave you; never will I forsake you" (Heb. 13:5). Even in disheartening circumstances, this verse reminds us we have reason to hope. The Lord is always with us; confidence in Him is never misplaced. No matter how lonely we may feel, we are never alone.

God is the God of hope. "May the God of hope fill you with all joy and peace as you trust in him, so that you may overflow with hope by the power of the Holy Spirit" (Rom. 15:13). As we trust in God and look to Him, God will fill us with joy and peace. Paul's desire was for the Christians to overflow with hope. More than anyone else in the world, Christians should be overflowing with hope, because we have a source of hope that is completely independent of our circumstances.

HEAVEN IS COMING

If we have no reason for optimism in this life, we can always look forward to what is coming in heaven. "Set your hope on the grace to be brought to you when Jesus Christ is revealed at his coming" (1 Pet. 1:13). The hope of heaven is one of the great joys of the Christian life.

I want to set my heart on the joy of heaven. "Blessed are you who weep now, for you will laugh. . . . Rejoice in that day and leap for joy, because great is your reward in heaven" (Luke 6:21, 23). In heaven, we will laugh. When I imagine heaven, I always get this picture in my head of sitting around a table with friends and us dying of laughter.

This life is short. Therefore, I want to be more consumed with loving the Lord, more consumed with His kingdom, and more consumed with loving people. I want to be less consumed with spending time thinking about if, how, when, and with whom this whole marriage thing might work out. Whatever way things work out, someday I will be in heaven laughing and rejoicing. Today I want my heart to rest in the picture of that day.

We love happy endings. Sometimes we need reassurance that our lives will have a happy ending. This is the verse I think about when I need to remind myself it will all be okay in the end. "I know that my redeemer lives, and that in the end he will stand on the earth" (Job 19:25). What really matters is that in the end I will be with Jesus.

Sometimes we need to look at the situation from more of an eternal perspective. From the Lord's perspective, we never have a reason to be hopeless. Hope is meant to be an anchor for our soul. Too often, however, our souls are only anchored in the prospect of things turning out the way we dreamed. God designed our souls to grasp something more enduring than the temporary. We need to anchor our souls in the truth of who the Lord is and in anticipation of the heaven He has prepared for us.

In order to keep my hope in the Lord steadfast, I need to renew my heart in the truth of Scripture. When I do not process my disappointments through the truth of Scripture, I end up questioning God. The words of the Bible are a great source of encouragement. The Bible helps me to see that whatever the Lord takes me through, I always have reason to trust in Him.

In the Bible, there is typically an action verb associated with hope. "Set" or "put" are the two most common. These words imply that we get to choose what we set our hope on or what we put our hope in. Let us set our hope on heaven, and let us put our hope in the Lord.

THE COMING WEDDING FEAST

We need to make sure we are setting our hope on the right thing. A man may never come for you and ask you to be his wife, but Jesus will come for you. Let us set our hope more on the day Christ comes for His bride than on being anyone else's bride. "As a young man marries a young woman, so will your Builder marry you; as a bridegroom rejoices over his bride, so will your God rejoice over you" (Isa. 62:5).

One thing that is certainly coming is the wedding feast of the Lamb. At least twice Jesus refers to this in His preaching. "The kingdom of heaven is like a king who prepared a wedding banquet for his son" (Matt. 22:2). "But while they were gone to buy oil, the bridegroom came. Then those who were ready went in with him to the marriage feast, and the door was locked" (Matt. 25:10 NLT). These verses alone are not enough to know that Jesus was alluding to a real event. The main reference for the coming wedding feast of the Lamb is in Revelation.

Then I heard what sounded like a great multitude, like the roar of rushing waters and like loud peals of thunder, shouting: "Hallelujah! For our Lord God Almighty reigns. Let us rejoice and be glad and give him glory! For the wedding of the Lamb has come, and his bride has made herself ready. Fine linen, bright and clean, was given her to wear." (Fine linen stands for the righteous acts of God's holy people.) Then the angel said to me, "Write this: Blessed are those who are invited to the wedding supper of the Lamb!" And he added, "These are the true words of God." (Rev. 19:6–9)

We may never get to have our dream wedding reception in this life. But even if we do not, this wedding feast will be far greater than any we have ever imagined for ourselves. Our hope needs to be set more on what is coming in heaven than on getting to plan a wedding here on earth. Not everyone who wants to get married will get married.

The more single women I talk to, the more I realize how much we all wrestle with putting too much hope in marriage. Sometimes I am surprised when I see the fulfillment of the verse: "No temptation has overtaken you except what is common to mankind" (1 Cor. 10:13). We all tend to think that our struggles are unique to us, and the people around us could not possibly relate. Staying silent about struggles makes it difficult for friends to encourage you. Whether it is trusting in the Lord or the other topics in this book, we could all use more encouragement. Being honest with friends also helps you to see where and when you are compromising.

Some of you need to reevaluate little ways you have been putting your hope in marriage. Maybe you need to buy some supplies for your kitchen, or a new bedspread, or maybe even a new bed. It would be great if we could wait until we get married to buy all these things, but I have found they only become little glaring reminders that I am not married. One way to not put our hope in marriage is to not wait to buy things we would expect to buy when we get married.

Some of us may get married, but we should not live with our hope set on it. We should make sure our hope is in the Lord and in heaven, not in life turning out the way we dreamed. Some of us may not get married, which is why our hope needs to be in something bigger than marriage. I long to see a generation of single women whose hope is firmly in the Lord.

NOTE: At the end of each chapter you will find a few questions to help you process through what you have read. I encourage you to grab a journal and *actually write out the answers*. The more effort you put into writing out your answers, the more you will get out of each chapter.

P.S. "I don't know" is not a valid answer. Some questions will require you to spend time and effort thinking and processing through your answer.

JOURNAL QUESTIONS

1. In what ways are you putting your hope in marriage?

2. Are there little things you can do this week to embrace singleness?

3. Do you believe you will go to heaven when you die? Why?

   (If you have any confusion or uncertainty about this please read the Appendix.)

4. What are you looking forward to most about heaven?

TWO

* * * * * *

DO I NEED A DIFFERENT PERSPECTIVE?

*In this life, we have an incomplete view
of God's dealings, seeing His plan only
half finished and underdeveloped. Yet
once we stand in the magnificent temple
of eternity, we will have the proper
perspective and will see everything fitting
gracefully together!*

J. R. Macduff

Different perspectives lead to different conclusions. Our position within a situation makes it difficult to have a good perspective. If we focus in on one small, specific element, we can feel comfortable with it. When we focus on more than that small element, we can begin to feel overwhelmed. We may try to see the bigger picture, but we do not realize that we are not thinking big enough.

This is like a camera lens. Camera lenses can focus on the foreground while the background remains blurry. Or, they can focus on the background while an object in the foreground becomes blurry. Zooming in and zooming out offers a change in perspective that changes where the focus lies. On hard days, we need to remember to zoom in or zoom out on our lives.

In singleness, we have trouble with perspective when we

look at our lives. It is easy for us to get stuck in the middle focusing neither on the foreground nor the background. We can get stuck on the idea of turning thirty, forty, or fifty and remaining single. Then we start to feel overwhelmed with panic, anxiety, or discouragement. In the moments when my emotions threaten to overwhelm me, I have found it helpful to remember to zoom in and zoom out. By zooming in on my day-to-day life, or by zooming out to more of an eternal perspective, I find I can reign in my emotions. As I gain perspective, I am even able to gain a sense of peace.

ZOOM IN

A sense of panic about singleness usually does not ensue in my normal day-to-day life. That is until I start thinking about the possibility of turning forty and still being single. Panic usually leads to fear, and fear usually lead us to make bad decisions. When the panic starts to rise from looking several years down the road, we need to remember to zoom in. Zooming in means to focus on the now while letting the background become blurry.

There are several things that I have found helpful to remember when zooming in. Reflecting on the past several weeks, months, and years can give me reassurance as I look ahead. One common thought, at least in my head, is how can I make it through the next ten years if I do not get married? I have this underlying feeling that I can't do it, or I won't make it. Before my emotions totally run away with me, I remember I have made it through the past ten years. While I do not walk around volunteering to remain single for the next ten years, if it happens, I do know the Lord's grace is sufficient to carry me through it. His grace has been sufficient for the past ten years, and it will continue to be for the next ten. Seeing how the Lord has brought me through these years gives me confidence as I look to the years ahead.

Many of us have days where making it through the next year seems overwhelming, let alone the next ten. I have had my fair share of those days. When getting through a specific amount of time feels impossible, shorten it. If the thought of making it through the next ten years seems comparable to climbing Mount Everest, then shorten it to a year. A year, at times, can even feel overwhelming. The thought of going another year with no changes to our circumstances is simply too much. In that case, think of making it through the month. Months go by so fast that sometimes we say, "Wow it is already the end of the month!" There can also be days when even making it through the next month feels difficult. So focus on the week, or if needed, focus on that day. Think of all the days that you have succeeded in making it through; certainly, you can make it through one more day. Even on the roughest days in singleness, I hope we believe we can at least make it through one more day.

We may face other trials where we are wondering how we are even going to make it through the day. In these cases, we may need to focus on getting through the next hour. If an hour feels too heavy, then focus on the next minute. Pray and ask the Lord to help you get through the next minute. Ask Him to give you grace and strength to keep going. Open your Bible and read a psalm. Anything that resonates with you, pray it. A minute will soon pass. Use it to remind yourself that you have made it through that minute and can make it through the next. If needed, spend the whole hour reading psalms and praying. Hour by hour, you can make it through the day.

When you read that last paragraph you might have thought I was being overly dramatic (or maybe you've been there). Count yourself blessed if getting through the day has never seemed overwhelming. Go ahead and file my piece of advice away in your mind for a future day when it may pertain to you. Trials can come out of nowhere, so it is good to have a game plan before moments of crisis arrive.

Another factor of zooming in is the importance of being present in our day-to-day lives. It may sound strange because you are physically present in your daily life. What I am referring to is being mentally present and emotionally engaged. People who have gone through difficult circumstances often mentally check out. Rather than processing the pain, they distract themselves in any possible way.

There is a wide range of ways in which we can distract ourselves from whatever is hard in life. Surfing the Internet, planning a trip, binge-watching Netflix, and pursuing hobbies are ways we can distract ourselves. In and of themselves, there is nothing wrong with any of these. Please do not think that I am saying that these things are always wrong. But they are all examples of things I have done to distract myself from painful realities in my life. These things can keep us from processing our emotions. They can also keep us from being present in our relationships. Some other ways people cope with painful circumstances can be sinful. Many addicts are trying to escape emotional pain. You will never experience emotional healing unless you process through your emotional pain. This begins by addressing wounds caused by what others have done or left undone, what you have done, and what God has done or not done. The way you internalize these events will impact your relationship with God and others.

I understand that sometimes checking out of our current realities can be attractive. However, this should not be our normal day-to-day lives. We miss out on cultivating our friendships and engaging with people around us. When you are hanging out with your friends, how much do you look at your smartphone? Sometimes sitting in silence is awkward or conversation is awkward. In order to avoid what is uncomfortable, we scroll through our phones. Having technology always at our fingertips gives us the ability to distract ourselves all the time. But Jesus and His disciples did not avoid what was uncomfortable. Deep friendships are forged when we embrace even what is awkward, and we do not let ourselves checkout. How can you be more present in the moment and love the people around you?

Zoom Out

For many of us zooming out is more natural than zooming in. We like to have a plan and vision for what our lives will look like ten years from now. However, fear and anxiety creep in when those plans seem like they will not happen. The issue is not that we neglect looking to the future, but that we are not looking far enough ahead. We need to zoom out and look not ten years down the road, but one hundred years. There is so much in this life that we are anxious about that will not matter one hundred years from now or one thousand years from now. Zooming out to consider our lives in light of eternity will give us a better perspective.

Our lives on this earth are temporary and brief in comparison to the rest of our lives in eternity. Imagine a string wrapping around the earth several times represents our entire existence. The portion of the string representing our years on this current earth would only be the first inch. The Bible compares our lives to a shadow, a breath, and a mist (Ps. 144:4; James 4:14). Whatever our current heartaches, trials, difficulties, or weaknesses, they are not forever. The weight of the next fifty years might feel like forever, but our feelings are deceptive. It is hard for us to wrap our minds around the next ten years being like a breath, let alone the next fifty. Nevertheless, I think that one thousand years from now we will look back and be in agreement that it was like a breath. We need to factor in the eternity that is coming for us as we live our lives here.

In Acts, Stephen gives a speech and he summarizes the life of Joseph. "Because the patriarchs were jealous of Joseph, they sold him as a slave into Egypt. But God was with him and rescued him from all his troubles. He gave Joseph wisdom and enabled him to gain the goodwill of Pharaoh king of Egypt. So Pharaoh made him ruler over Egypt and all his palace" (Acts 7:9–10). If you are familiar with the life of Joseph, then you might realize what Stephen leaves out. The part where Joseph is falsely accused of rape and thrown in prison for years is merely implied in "all his troubles." He was in prison for years, even though he was innocent. I marvel at how easy it is to look back at the gut-wrenchingly hard parts of someone else's life and sum them up in three words.

Even as we look back at our lives, there are years we chunk together. I talk about how I was in college ministry for five years. There were many hard things that happened in those five years. I had moments where I wondered how people could continue following the Lord for twenty years. As I look back on those years, they do not seem as hard now as they felt in the moment.

Like Joseph experienced, our circumstances can seem like a hopeless prison. When we are unsure if things will ever change, we need to remember the eternal picture. If we lose sight of the bigger picture, we can become overwhelmed in the middle of what we are experiencing. I am sure there were days when Joseph was in jail where he was extremely discouraged. After he had been there for years, there was still no end in sight. He probably wondered if anything would ever change or if he would ever get out of that prison. One day everything quickly changed and Pharaoh released Joseph. When Stephen summarized Joseph's life, the years in prison are not even mentioned.

It is key for us to remember that our current circumstances are not forever. Everything can change quickly. When life feels overwhelming, we need to remember that looking back five years from now, we may sum it all up with three words: "It was hard." Even if our circumstances do not change before we die, they are not forever. For Christians, our forever is in the new heaven and the new earth with the Lord.

There are some hardships in life that will not end before we are with the Lord. Paul was aware of this when he wrote to the Christians, "We boast about your perseverance and faith in all the persecutions and trials you are enduring . . . He will . . . give relief to you who are troubled, and to us as well. This will happen when the Lord Jesus is revealed from heaven" (2 Thess. 1:4, 6, 7). He encourages them that the Lord will give relief from trials and persecutions, but it will not necessarily happen in this life. Relief will come to all believers when Jesus is revealed in the end. Relief is coming. The Lord will give relief from the trials of life when we stand before Him and see Him face-to-face. Paul does not give them some fluffy statement of false hope that they will be given relief from trials in this life. He encourages them to set their sights not on the trial in front of them, but on the day they will see Jesus. The hope of the day when we will see the Lord can give us the strength to endure hardships and trials in this life.

One key to following the Lord and to preserving in trials is to zoom out. In view of eternity, this life is short. "For this world in its present form is passing away" (1 Cor. 7:31). The Lord wants us to have a bigger view because this life is temporary and passing away. We need to set our sights on heaven and on the day we will see the Lord. When we set our sights on building our dream lives here, we get too engrossed in the things of this world. Forever and ever is the span of our lives in heaven. I am not sure we can grasp the weight of eternity on this side where everything is temporary. Nevertheless, I am trying to focus on the eternal. I want to look ahead to a forever where, "Gladness and joy will overtake them, and sorrow and sighing will flee away" (Isa. 35:10). I do not want to get lost in seeking a temporary "happily ever after" here. I often do not give enough thought to looking ahead one hundred years in order to consider what will last forever.

It is odd, in a way, that I know more about my life one hundred years from now than I know about my life ten years from now. Compiling verses on heaven gives me a picture of what my life will look like in eternity, but there is no description of my life ten years from now. Amid the uncertainty of what the next ten years will hold, my heart can rest in the certainty of heaven.

As we live our lives here we need to remember that heaven is coming. Trials, pain, and hardships are only a part of our lives here. The Lord does not only see our current circumstances. If we put our faith and trust in the Lord, He sees us one hundred years from now in heaven. He sees us enjoying a perfect relationship with Him and perfect relationships with friends and family. We need to strive to zoom out, to look beyond our current circumstances, and to seek to catch a glimpse of eternity.

Our perspective impacts how we view our circumstances. It can be overwhelming to think of going through the next twenty years and never getting married. In moments when it is overwhelming that our circumstances might not change anytime soon, we need to remember to zoom in and zoom out. Zoom in on whatever time frame feels less overwhelming to you and look to the Lord to help you through it. Zoom out by remembering that even if your circumstances never change in this life, this life is not forever. Do not lose sight of heaven. In a little while, there will be a day when the pain of this life will melt away and we will be in His presence.

JOURNAL QUESTIONS

1. In moments when you feel overwhelmed, what key things have you found helpful to remember?
2. Why is it helpful to reflect on the things we have made it through?
3. In what ways do you avoid facing difficult relationships, situations, or emotions?
4. What emotional wounds do you still carry from your past? How have they influenced your perception of how God feels about you and how you feel about Him?

5. What is your favorite verse that reminds you that life is short? Why is it helpful to remember that this life is temporary?

THREE

* * * * * *

WHAT AM I FEEDING MY SOUL?

*Friend, if you were as good at soul-cultivation
as you are in developing your business, you
would be a menace to the devil; but if you were
as poor in business matters as you are in soul,
you would be begging for bread.*

Leonard Ravenhill, *Why Revival Tarries*

One of my greatest desires is to still be following the Lord when I get to the end of my life. Over the years, I have seen people who were following the Lord, who are not anymore. This is not a new thing. In the Old Testament, there were many kings who started following the Lord but did not finish well. Whatever life does or does not hold, I want to finish well.

Trials come in all shapes and sizes. If you have been single far longer than you ever wished, then you may consider singleness to be a trial. I know I would. However, if I were ranking my trials by difficulty, it would not make the top ten. While not the most difficult, it has been the longest trial in my life, stretching over a decade. The longer a trial goes on, the more it weighs on us.

Trials, and sometimes life in general, wear me out. Some days even my soul feels weary. Often on those days, my first thought regarding a remedy is that I need time to vedge. I need to relax by sitting on a couch and binge-watching the night away on Netflix. Netflix does provide a great escape from the reality of my life. The trouble is it does not do much to refresh my heart, restore my soul, or encourage my spirit. The next day my soul still feels weary.

Recently, I have been thinking about this question: What are we feeding our souls? If I want to follow the Lord until I die, then what can I do to encourage myself to keep going? This prompted me to reflect on what things have been the most encouraging to me spiritually since I started following Christ. In the same way that what we eat impacts our physical health, what we feed our souls impacts our spiritual health.

When trials are overwhelming, we need to incorporate things into our schedule that refresh our souls. I do not think these should only be a priority when life is hard. We should do them regularly to stay encouraged and to prepare for whatever lies ahead.

THE WORD

First and foremost, my most constant source of encouragement is the Bible. When I went to college I started going to a Bible study that met in the lobby of my dorm. Many of the older students leading the group read the Bible every day and encouraged me to do the same. They read the one-year Bible reading plan, so I started reading it too. That first year I had many epiphanies as I discovered there was so much in the Bible I never thought would be in there.

I had tried to read the Bible in high school but never managed to get very far. One reason it was easier for me to read the Bible in college was that my time was my own. In singleness, we have more freedom in deciding how to use our time, or at least fewer people chiming in about what we should do. We have an opportunity to spend time seeking the Lord.

The Bible reveals the character and nature of God. If we are going to trust the Lord through difficulties, we must be confident that we know the One in whom we are trusting. The most spiritual growth in my life has come as a result of reading the Bible daily. The more you read, the more you will grow in your knowledge and understanding of truth. There is such a rich depth to the Bible. I have read through the entire Bible more than ten times, and I still learn new things each time.

The main reason the Bible feeds and encourages my soul is because it reminds me who the Lord is when the road ahead is dark. As human beings sometimes we are so forgetful—half the time I do not remember what I did last week. I need to remind myself of who the Lord is and what He has done for me because I often lose sight of it in the craziness of life. The more I lose sight of it, the more prone I am to wander away from the Lord and into sin (believing He is withholding good things from me). When life explodes in your face, it is hard to remember what is true. In those moments, we need to cling to the truth in the Bible, but that is much easier to do if you are already very familiar with it and already have a habit of reading it daily.

It was the Bible that carried me through the hardest days of my life. Before those days, the Word of God was already precious to me. I had my favorite passages marked, so I knew where to turn in the Bible. You should not wait until life gets hard to start reading because you will not even be sure where to start. There will be some other habit you have built into your life as a source of comfort and that is where you will turn. We need to consider what we feed our souls daily, so we know where to look when we are weary and need extra nourishment. In a psalm, it says the Word of God: refreshes the soul, makes wise the simple, gives joy to the heart, and gives light to the eyes (Ps. 19:7, 8). These are all things I need more of in my life. The habit of turning to the Bible is something we need to ingrain into our lives.

I once heard about this old lady who had read through the entire Bible seventy times. We did not use hashtags at that time, but now I would say: *#lifegoals*. If you have never read the entire Bible, I would challenge you to get a one-year Bible reading plan. For the past several years, I have read the one-year chronological plan. In case you did not know, the books of the Old Testament are not completely in the order of when they happened. I prefer to read through it in the order in which the events happened. The hard part is finding a chronological plan where you read both the Old and New Testament every day. It is generally better to read a little from both, especially on the days when you feel the Old Testament is boring. If you read three chapters in the Old Testament and one chapter in the New Testament every day, you will read the whole Bible in a year.

If the Old Testament seems daunting to you, I would encourage you to try reading it anyway. I started it when I was an eighteen-year-old who knew next to nothing. The first time I read through the Old Testament, I did not understand a lot of it. Every time I read through it, there is less and less I do not understand. Avoiding reading it will not help you grow in understanding it.

If you are too overwhelmed to attempt to read the whole Bible in a year, then start with the New Testament and Psalms. If you have never even read through the whole New Testament, then this is a simple and great way to start. Start in Matthew and read one chapter every day until you get to the end of the New Testament. Once you get to the end, I hope you will try to read through the entire Bible. In addition to one chapter in the New Testament, read one Psalm. You should be able to read through Psalms twice a year. If you are thinking, "I do not have time to read the Bible," I have a suggestion that might help with the issue of finding time. Unplug the Wi-Fi in your house and turn off the data on your phone every night before you go to bed. Do not reconnect them the next day until you have read the Bible. With no Internet, it will be surprising the amount of time that appears out of nowhere. I am amazed at the amount of time I waste scrolling through newsfeeds.

One of the most important things we can do to feed our souls is to spend rich time in the Bible every day. Moses said, "Man does not live on bread alone but on every word that comes from the mouth of the Lord" (Deut. 8:3). No one would think they could be physically healthy and properly nourished by eating once a week. No one would say: "I ate every day last year, so I can skip eating this year." Somehow Christians are often deceived into thinking this line of thought spiritually. In my personal opinion, reading less than one chapter in the New Testament and one Psalm a day is a starvation diet. Sadly our souls can be spiritually starving, but we do not realize it. Many do not realize it because they do not know what it is like to be well fed.

PRAYER

The longer I have been following the Lord, the more encouragement I have found from going on prayer walks. The building where I work is next to a public bike trail. The trail goes through a small wooded area with a creek running alongside it. One of my favorite things to do is to take a late lunch break and pray while walking on this trail. I pray about a variety of things: family, friends, and life circumstances. The greatest refreshment seems to come when I pray about whatever is heavy on my heart. "Pour out your hearts to him" (Ps. 62:8 NLT). The more painful my circumstances are, the sweeter my times in prayer are to my soul.

When my soul feels heavy, what I need the most is to process what is going on in my life and heart with the Lord. The longer I remain single, the more I have to pray about it and verbally entrust my life and heart to the Lord. Prayer walks are usually where I hash out all my angst. A good chunk of the thoughts in this book came out of spending time both in the Word and in prayer. I find praying over the verses that stick out to me while reading is an encouragement to my soul.

If you have never gone on a prayer walk, then this idea might seem a bit strange to you. In college, I would pray silently in my head as I walked between classes. I also went on prayer walks with a friend around campus. The second place I pray the most is in my car. I stay more focused on praying when I talk aloud. Praying for my closest friends on my drive to work is a habit I started years ago, and I still continue to this day. Praying aloud in your car is more private than praying aloud while walking down the sidewalk.

One time last year, I was praying aloud while walking on

the bike trail, and I was praying louder than usual (the volume I might use to carry on a conversation with someone on the far side of a room). Suddenly I realized there was a man right next to me who was walking a little faster than me and was passing me. I quickly stopped praying but he must have heard me. It was my awkward turtle moment of the week. If you are not willing to try praying outside aloud, then find some other place to spend time in prayer. How would your relationship with the Lord deepen if you took the time you normally spend wallowing in Netflix and spent it in prayer?

FRIENDS

At times following Jesus can feel like a lonely road. Following Jesus in singleness can feel like an even lonelier road. Even though I am a total introvert, I love sitting down with other women to talk about life and the Bible. It helps me to process what I am reading when I share my thoughts with another person. Sharing what we are reading in the Bible is one of the best ways that we can "encourage one another daily" (Heb. 3:13).

These times with friends and these conversations do not happen by accident though. In order for them to happen regularly, someone needs to be willing to initiate. Honestly, sometimes women make me want to pull my hair out. I am a woman, so I can say that, right? No one wants to take the initiative to ask a friend out to coffee, lunch, or dinner. Everyone wants to have their friends ask them to hang out. They may be willing to ask someone one time, but then it is the other person's turn to initiate and ask them. Only this is never communicated and the other person has no idea that it is "their turn." This typically leads to people hanging out less and feeling lonely more.

I have found that singleness feels less lonely when I am regularly hanging out with friends. In order to have coffee, go out to lunch, or have dinner with women on a regular basis I have to be willing to initiate every time. My favorite weeks are weeks where I have a couple of coffee dates, lunch dates, and dinner dates. But I've learned that if I do not ask other women, these will never happen. Too often women can internalize no one asking them to hang out to mean that no one cares about them. This is not the case; women are just bad initiators.

If you have friends who you have not spent time with in a while, then you should text them and ask them when they are free. If there are women who you would like to know better, then you need to be willing to text them and ask them out to coffee. Also, you should assume you will need to text them next time in order to hang out with them in the future. In college, it was easier to always be hanging out with people. I have found the older I get, the more intentional I have to be to initiate with other women.

When we talk with people, we also need to be willing to change the topic to a more spiritual direction. It is easy to sit and have superficial conversations about general things in life. Sometimes we need to risk being a little awkward and ask them deeper spiritual questions. My favorite conversations are when we share what we are learning in the Bible, small group, or church. In singleness, deep friendships are so important, but again they will not happen accidentally. We must continue to initiate with women in order to cultivate these close friendships.

CHURCH AND SMALL GROUP BIBLE STUDY

The fellowship, worship, and sermons that are a part of a church service are additional things that encourage my soul. Singing praises to the Lord always helps me to rejoice in what He has already done for me. It is a blessing to hear godly men preach and remind me of biblical truth. They offer nuggets of wisdom that they have acquired from years of serving the Lord. Church also provides an opportunity to connect with others and meet new people.

One way most churches have for us to connect with others is through small groups. Whether it is a co-ed or women-only Bible study, these groups offer discussions on a variety of topics. It is a chance to hear different perspectives and to build deeper friendships. Small groups allow others to encourage our souls. It also gives us an opportunity to encourage and build into others. When you have been part of small group long enough, they often begin to feel more like family than friends. Overtime, you will laugh together, cry together, mourn together, rejoice together, and eat a lot of food together. As singles, if we live far away from our families, these friends that are like family are a blessing to our lives and an asset in fighting loneliness.

God intends Christians to be in fellowship with one another. Jesus said, "By this everyone will know that you are my disciples, if you love one another" (John 13:35). If we do not see each other, it is going to make it difficult to live out loving one another. Jesus's desire is that we would live this out in such a way that when the world sees it, they would know we are His followers. This means we need to commit to being in community with other believers. In this community, we should seek to "spur one another on toward love and good deeds" (Heb. 10:24).

CONFERENCES AND RETREATS

The concept for this chapter came while I was attending an annual church conference. Many friends have attended this conference with me over the years, but every year less of them come back. They are still following the Lord, but attending this conference is no longer a priority. I understand that once you have listened to messages at conferences, retreats, and church for over ten years there is very little new information. However, I want to go to this conference every year for as long as it continues to exist.

At the conference, I pushed my sleeping baby nephew around in a stroller. My brother-in-law, who is a pastor, gave a breakout session talk, and my sister went to listen to her husband teach. I volunteered to watch the baby and wandered the halls of the convention center. As I thought about why continuing to come to this conference is so important to me, the answer became clear: because it feeds and encourages my soul. Even if everything is not new information, it is great to get away from my normal schedule for three days of undistracted worship and teaching. It refocuses my heart and re-centers my life on the Lord. These three days offer some of the best food I can feed my soul.

MAKE A PLAN

I will feed my soul something every day, every week, every month, and every year. At the same time the world will also feed my soul, but it is not likely to be food that nourishes me spiritually. As the years pass by, we do not automatically grow more spiritually mature. The only thing that happens automatically is we grow older. I want to be intentional about feeding myself good things that will help me grow spiritually.

Reading the Bible is something I want and need to incorporate daily. Throughout my week, I want to schedule times with friends and time in prayer. Fellowship at church and small group are important to refresh my soul every week. They also give me an opportunity to be a blessing and encouragement to others. There are events like conferences, retreats, and mission trips that refocus my heart. These I desire to continue to incorporate into my life every year.

Very few, if any, of these things, will happen randomly and on their own. If I do not make a plan and stick to it, then I find my soul starting to drift. "But the noble make noble plans, and by noble deeds they stand" (Isa. 32:8). The wearier my soul feels, the more faithful I need to be in incorporating these things into my schedule. In singleness, there is an additional sense of disappointment and pain from my life not turning out the way I expected. This means I need to be all the more intentional about encouraging my soul. Every day I will store up something in my soul. I need a plan to store up what is good. If I want to finish well, then I need to feed my soul well.

JOURNAL QUESTIONS

1. What things do you do on a regular basis that *don't* encourage your soul?
2. Why do you do these things?
3. What things do you do (or want to do) on a regular basis that would encourage your soul?

4. Why do you do them? Why do you want to do them?

5. How can you intentionally build into your schedule more of the things that encourage your soul?

FOUR

* * * * * *

Does God See Me?

It seems to have been a mistake to imagine that the Divine Majesty on high was too exalted to take notice of our mean affairs. The great minds among men are remarkable for the attention they bestow on minutiae.

David Livingstone

Each one of us wants to know someone sees us. We hate feeling ignored. We may have moments we wish to be invisible, but we do not want to be invisible to everybody all the time. When we are in emotional pain, we want to hide it from some people, but we also want others to notice our pain.

If we see other people in pain, we want to do what we can to ease their pain. Surely, if God sees me, He would want to do what He could to ease my pain. When my hardships do not end though, I begin to question if God sees me and my pain, because if He did, He would surely not let this continue. Some days all I want is my circumstances to be different. I want my trials and difficulties to be over. Extended, painful trials create an impression that God does not see me.

In my head, I know God's heart, and I know He sees all. I can be confident of God's heart toward me, for a while, but then I will have moments where my emotions overwhelm me. Moments where I recognize that in the depths of my soul I am questioning if God sees me, loves me, or cares for me at all. My circumstances seem to be strong evidence that He does not.

Singleness is one of the hardships that can cause me to doubt God's heart toward me. As my desire for marriage remains unfulfilled, some days I am unable to shake the feeling of being unseen. It is as if I am jumping up and down, waving my arms back and forth, yelling at the sky, and getting no response. Surely this must testify that He does not see me. He may have noticed me at one time, but now I have been forgotten.

As friend after friend get married and we get older, there is a feeling that we are being overlooked. If we are being overlooked by men, then maybe we are also being overlooked by God. On second thought, wishing to be invisible might not be such a good idea after all.

In my wrestling with believing that God's heart toward me is full of loving-kindness, He is always gracious to remind me of what is true. I want to cling to what is true, ingrain it in my mind, and bury it in my heart. This has led me to intentionally dwell on truth about each area where I tend to question God's heart.

HAGAR'S STORY

For many years when I read through Genesis, I would pass over Hagar and focus on Sarah. Hagar did not seem important because her child was not the promised child. Sarah had the promised child, so I would focus on her. A few years ago, though, the story of Hagar captured my attention. The verses about Hagar have now become my favorite verses in the entire book of Genesis. The full story of Hagar is found in Genesis 16 and 21.

When Genesis 16 starts, it had been over ten years since God first told Abram that he would become a great nation. Sarai—her name has not yet changed to Sarah, had been unable to conceive a child. She thought they had waited on the Lord long enough—and she began to see what she could do to help move things along. Hagar was her slave, and Sarai decided to have her husband, Abram, sleep with Hagar in order to try to give him a son (this was not such an uncommon practice back then). Much to Hagar's dismay, she became pregnant, and she despised Sarai for it. Sarai then mistreated Hagar, and Hagar decided to run away.

Emotionally, Hagar was a mess. She was angry and hurt about the circumstances of her life. This was not her dream. This was not her plan. This was not the life she wanted. Running away seemed like a good idea, so she left. She was in the desert by a spring wallowing in the misery that nothing seemed to be going her way.

An angel of the Lord met her there and asked her a two-part question, "Hagar, slave of Sarai, where have you come from, and where are you going?" (Gen. 16:8). Hagar responded, "I'm running away from my mistress Sarai" (Gen. 16:8). Notice, Hagar only answered the first question. All she knew was that she was running away from her current circumstances. She did not seem to have had a plan for where she was going to go. She simply wanted to go somewhere else, so her life could be different. Running away to the desert while pregnant was not the best life plan. Her heart was in so much pain, though, she did not think about that; she just ran.

I have moments where I want to run away from the circumstances of my life. Days where I wake up wishing the trials in my life were all a bad dream. Days where my eyes are tired of crying. Days where I wonder why staying curled up in a ball in bed all day is not a legitimate option. This is not what I signed up for. This is not the life I envisioned. We all have hard days, but as days stretch into months or years, the weight of it all presses in on us. Like Hagar, we can want to go somewhere else, or do something else. Anywhere. Anything. As long as it means our life is different. When life turns out not to be all we dreamed, there can be a strong desire to run: to run from the pain. Staying means facing the painful reality of our lives. If only we could outrun the pain in our hearts. But, if we run, the pain will follow. This world is full of people trying to escape pain.

When we are in emotional pain, it feels as though no one sees us. In facing pain, we are often the most isolated. The voice in our heads seems to shout, "God does not see you! He is not paying attention to you! He is overlooking you! He is turning his back on you!"

As I reflect on the story of Hagar, it is the Lord's heart that stands out to me. She was in a place where she thought no one saw her, and no one cared for her. But the Lord saw Hagar. The Lord even pursued Hagar. He spoke tenderly to her. She probably felt so alone, but the Lord noticed her. He came and met her in her brokenness and confusion.

The Lord's heart toward us is the same. On days when it feels like God does not see us, we need to remember His heart toward Hagar. We need to recognize God sees us and meets us in our brokenness.

Hagar was sitting on the ground. Her heart was heavy

and she was not sure what to do next. The angel also gave her several promises about her unborn child. The most significant thing the angel said to her was, "For the Lord has heard of your misery" (Gen. 16:11). The God of the Universe revealed to her that He knew her, He saw her, and He was aware of her misery. He saw what she was going through and He cared for her.

The angel of the Lord also told her, "Go back to your mistress and submit to her" (Gen. 16:9). Even though none of her circumstances had changed, she chose to go back to Sarah and Abraham. The only difference now was she had a new understanding that God saw her. Her knowing and believing that God saw her changed everything. After the angel spoke to her, she responded, "You are the God who sees me . . . I have now seen the One who sees me" (Gen. 16:13). Hagar's heart was so moved by this moment, she named the well Beer Lahai Roi, which means *well of the Living One who sees me* (Gen. 16:14). Knowing the Living One saw her gave her strength to walk back into the circumstances she ran away from.

Many days, the only thing we want is for our circumstances to change—as if we could find life in a different set of circumstances. The Lord knows there is something we need more than "a change." What we actually need is a closer relationship with Him, a deeper awareness of His presence, and a greater trust in His character. We find life in a relationship with God. Sometimes our relationship with God only grows closer, deeper, and stronger through hardship. Processing our pain with the Lord allows our relationship with Him to grow sweeter.

When we understand that the Lord sees our pain, it helps

us to persevere through trials. "I trust in the Lord . . . for you saw my affliction and knew the anguish of my soul" (Ps. 31:6–7). Hagar goes back to the same circumstances because she understands that God sees her affliction and knows her anguish.

Hagar's story does not end with her returning to Sarah and Abraham. It continues in Genesis 21. After Sarah gave birth to Isaac, Sarah requested that Hagar and Ishmael leave. Abraham gave them some food and water and sent them on their way. After wandering around in the desert, they ran out of food and water. The child was crying, and Hagar thought he was going to die. Then the angel of the Lord spoke to her and opened her eyes to see a well of water.

God continued to show His love and faithfulness to Hagar. When she lost all hope, God came to the rescue; He provided for her deepest needs. He saw her pain and her thirst, and He provided refreshment. The remarkable thing was that Hagar was an Egyptian slave. She was neither of special birth nor position; she was a "nobody." In the same way, neither do we need to be of special birth nor position for God to see us. God revealed Himself to Hagar. He is also revealing Himself to you through the account of what happened in her life. God is revealing that He is a God who sees the misery in your life.

One key to persevering through difficult trials is to believe that God sees you. He sees your pain. He sees your heartache. He sees what is hard, unjust, and unfair. "Does he who fashioned the ear not hear? Does he who formed the eye not see?" (Ps. 94:9). Far be it from the realm of possibility that He who formed the eye would Himself be unable to see. Rest assured He is not blind to your pain nor your suffering.

Are you convinced of that? Have you ever considered that the very circumstances you want to run away from might be the exact ones that God wants you to be in?

Sometimes knowing and believing that He sees our lives is all we need to press on and finish the race. At least, I have found it encouraging on hard days. For as long as God wants me to be single, I want to trust that He is not overlooking me.

NOT FORGOTTEN

Even though I want to trust Him, I still have days where I wrestle with my feelings, and I need to remind myself of what is true. It is reassuring to know that I am not the first to feel forgotten by the Lord. "But Zion said, 'The Lord has forsaken me, the Lord has forgotten me'" (Isa. 49:14). The people of Jerusalem felt the Lord had forgotten them. When we feel forgotten, we need to remember what the Lord said to them: "Can a mother forget the baby at her breast and have no compassion on the child she has borne? Though she may forget, I will not forget you! See, I have engraved you on the palms of my hands; your walls are ever before me" (Isa. 49:15–16). We are never forgotten; He engraved us on the palms of His hands. Suffering is not evidence that God has forgotten us.

There is a pain and difficulty that comes with suffering, especially when it feels unjust. "For it is commendable if someone bears up under the pain of unjust suffering because they are conscious of God" (1 Pet. 2:19). It is interesting that a key to bearing up under the pain of unjust suffering is to be conscious of God. Oftentimes people's consciousness of God makes them bitter toward Him. He either caused their suffering or He could have prevented it, but did not. However, it is also our awareness of God that helps us bear up under immense pressure. We can bear the pain if we are conscious that He sees our pain. It is more than simply that He sees us, though: *He is with us*. He upholds us in it (Isa. 41:10). He carries us through it (Isa. 46:4). He might not take us out of a hard situation, but He will be with us in it—always (Matt. 28:20).

Not only does God see us, but He also sees better than we do. He sees our lives now, ten years from now, and twenty years from now. "He who forms the hearts of all, who considers everything they do" (Ps. 33:15). He formed my heart, knows my heart, and considers my heart. He considers my life and everything I do, but He considers more than only me. He sees all human beings; I only see myself. I would understand the ways of the Lord a bit more if I could see the bigger picture the way He does. We do not see everything; we only see in part.

From our viewpoint life is not turning out the way we planned. We often do not see the opportunities that we have (and would not otherwise have) if life were going according to our plans. Looking back, sometimes we can see we were touching lives in ways we would not have if our dreams had come true. In the moment, we usually do not recognize how God is using us. We see our unfulfilled dreams. We struggle to imagine the good in it, or how God can use it.

God sees it all. He knows the hearts and lives we can touch because of our current circumstances. He considers the things we now have the opportunities to do. He sees the thread of our lives intertwining with the lives of so many others. There might be a purpose to our singleness that we are not yet aware of.

On hard days, it encourages my heart to remember that Jesus notices me every single day. He never overlooks me. The Lord sees me and knows exactly how old I am. He does not forget me nor forget my age. He knows all the details of my life. If He wants me to wait several more years before I marry or even if I never marry, it is all in His hands. He sees me and is not overlooking me.

JOURNAL QUESTIONS

1. When have you felt unseen and overlooked by God?
2. In what ways do you identify with Hagar? Have you ever had the desire to run away from your circumstances?
3. Why might God have placed you in those circumstances? Or allowed them?
4. What other verses remind you that God sees you and the details of your life? How often do you intentionally dwell on this truth?
5. Why do you think it is important to believe that God sees you?
6. How has hardship caused your relationship with God to grow closer, deeper, and stronger?

FIVE

* * * * * *

DOES GOD CARE ABOUT ME?

*Here I was worrying about my journey,
while God was helping me all the way.
I made me realize that I am very weak; my
courage is only borrowed from Him, but,
oh, the peace that flooded my soul . . .
because I know that He never faileth.*

Gladys Aylward

The wind whips across my face. In a little while, my cheeks will go numb, and it will not sting as much. I am bundled up so well, my eyes and cheeks are the only things exposed. The bike path is empty. It is only me, my thoughts, and God. It is far too cold for the other people I often see out here. If only the cold wind could make the emotions churning in my heart as numb as it makes my cheeks.

Thoughts swirl around in my head. I know they are not true. Accusations against the Lord reverberate around my mind. *He does not care when my heart aches. He does not care how long He leaves me in my misery. He does not care that my day feels heavier than I can bear.*

My heart echoes with the desire of the psalmist. "'Oh, that I had the wings of a dove! I would fly away and be at rest. I would flee far away and stay in the desert'" (Ps. 55:6–7). If only I had wings like a bird and could fly away from my circumstances. I wish I could fly away from my troubles, my sorrows, and the hardships that press against me in this life. It would be great if I could go away on vacation and come back to every issue having resolved itself. If I did have the wings of a bird, I would not fly to the desert. I would fly to the mountains or the beach. But I am not a bird. Instead, I walk on a path through the woods.

My thoughts turn to a familiar Bible passage: the disciples caught in the storm as they crossed the lake. They found themselves questioning whether Jesus cared. As the storm grew worse, Jesus kept sleeping. The disciples shook Him awake saying, "'Teacher, don't you care if we drown?'" (Mark 4:38). When trials threaten to drown us, in our gut there can be a growing fear that He does not care.

I keep walking on the path, because it is too cold to sit on my usual bench. I hear no voice, but the wind seems to whisper back the Lord's response to my accusations. *I am anything but indifferent. I am not apathetic. My heart aches more than you can grasp. I bled so you would know how much I care.*

I walk in silence as I contemplate the truth in those words. Jesus's blood was not shed because He was unconcerned about our lives. Still, my heart goes back-and-forth. One minute it is resting in quiet confidence of God, and the next it is slinging pointed questions at Him.

When we wrestle with doubts, we need to be intentional in seeking to remind ourselves what is true. The devil loves it when we question God and do not remember the truth. Israel strayed from the Lord in the Old Testament because they failed to remember. They failed to remember who the Lord was and what He had done for them.

My favorite book in the Chronicles of Narnia series is *The Silver Chair*. Aslan sends the children on a quest. He gives them four signs to remember. If they can remember these four signs, the signs will be a great help on their quest. Aslan gives a warning, because remembering is not as easy as it sounds:

> But, first, remember, remember, remember the signs. Say them to yourself when you wake in the morning and when you lie down at night, and when you wake in the middle of the night. And whatever strange things may happen to you, let nothing turn your mind from following the signs. And secondly, I give you a warning. Here on the mountain I have spoken to you clearly: I will not often do so down in Narnia. Here on the mountain, the air is clear and your mind is clear; as you drop down into Narnia, the air will thicken. Take great care that it does not confuse your mind. And the signs which you have learned here will not look at all as you expect them to look, when you meet them there. That is why it is so important to know them by heart and pay no attention to appearances. Remember the signs and believe the signs. Nothing else matters.[1]

If you have never read that book, the children struggle to remember the signs. Like them, we fail to remember many things that God has told us. In the haziness of life, our minds become confused. When we are unable to distinguish truth from lies, our feelings and emotions cause us to doubt even more. We make bad choices if we decide based on what feels true in the moment. This usually leads us to do something that we otherwise would not do. It can be easy to lose sight of what is true in the confusion of this world. We need to remember and believe what God says is true.

Different things can prompt us to remember or think of something else. Tea reminds me of my grandmother, a tractor reminds me of my dad, and an aquarium reminds me of my brother. We can also create prompts that remind us of certain things. In school as I studied, I would create acronyms to think about during tests to help me remember the answers. In the same way, we all need prompts to help us remember what God tells us is true.

When our doubts begin to rise, there are deeper truths that we need to remember to consider. My advice to you is: Consider the birds.

Every month last year I read through the gospel of Luke. This served as a continuous reminder in my life to consider the birds. It is a tweak on what Jesus said to His disciples:

> Therefore I tell you, do not worry about your life, what you will eat; or about your body, what you will wear. For life is more than food, and the body more than clothes. Consider the ravens: They do not sow or reap; they have no storeroom or barn; yet

God feeds them. And how much more valuable you are than birds! Who of you by worrying can add a single hour to your life? Since you cannot do this very little thing, why do you worry about the rest? (Luke 12:22–26)

Jesus told His disciples to consider the ravens. They do not worry about the future, storing away food in barns; the Lord cares for them and takes care of them. We can slide into adopting the world's mentality that no one else will take care of us, so we must take care of ourselves. It is easy for us to worry about what we need and want and try to find any possible way to make it happen. We lose sight of the fact that the Lord supports us and takes care of us. He often does this in many ways we never even see. Sometimes we perceive what the Lord does for us, but countless times we are oblivious. When life is difficult, our emotions tend to blind us. The Lord tells us He cares for the ravens, and He provides for the ravens. He also tells us that we are much more valuable to Him than the birds. And if the Lord looks after the birds, will He not even more so care and provide for you?

There are several verses where Jesus uses birds as an example to demonstrate that God cares for us. The Lord did not communicate this in only one way. It is as if He knows we are prone to doubt, so He is looking for a million different ways to communicate that He cares. "Are not five sparrows sold for two pennies? Yet not one of them is forgotten by God. Indeed, the very hairs of your head are all numbered. Don't be afraid; you are worth more than many sparrows" (Luke 12:6–7). Sparrows sell for only a few pennies. They are not valuable. Nobody cares much about a few pennies. Even though sparrows are not worth much, not a single one of them is ever forgotten by God. God notices every single sparrow. Surely, if God does not forget about a single sparrow, He does not forget a single one of us either. We are worth so much more than many sparrows. If He cares for the sparrows, how much more does He care about you? He cares so much for you that He numbers all the hairs on your head.

When you feel doubts creep into your heart, remember to consider the ravens and the sparrows. I do not know how to tell the difference between a raven and a crow. To me a sparrow is a small bird like most birds. For simplicity sake, I have condensed it to: Consider the birds. When I am on a prayer walk on the bike trail through the woods, I see a lot of birds. They have become a symbolic reminder to me. They remind me that even when the circumstances of my life do not change, the Lord still cares for me. The depth of the Lord's care for me is more than I can imagine, and singleness is not evidence that the Lord does not care about me.

THE LORD PROVIDES

The Bible is full of countless examples of God's care and provision for people. In 1 Kings, Elijah places the land under a drought, and God tells Elijah to hide from the king until it is time for the drought to end.

> Then the word of the Lord came to Elijah: "Leave here, turn eastward and hide in the Kerith Ravine, east of the Jordan. You will drink from the brook, and I have directed the ravens to supply you with food there."

> So he did what the Lord had told him. He
> went to the Kerith Ravine, east of the
> Jordan, and stayed there. The ravens
> brought him bread and meat in the morning
> and bread and meat in the evening, and he
> drank from the brook. (1 Kings 17:2–6)

Elijah stays here by this brook until it dries up, and twice a day the ravens bring him food, as directed by the Lord. In this example, the Lord is not providing for the ravens, but instead is using the ravens to demonstrate His ability to take care of Elijah. Our God cares for His people, and He will take care of them. This is a reminder for us that God's arm is never too short to provide.

However, it is when He feels slow in providing that I begin to doubt. Especially, if it seems like He is not going to come through. Perceptions, however, are deceiving. I need to continue to remember God's heart towards me in order to rest in His care and provision.

There is so little, in a sense, that I am unable to provide for myself. I know everything I have is from the Lord, and my ability to provide for myself is a blessing from the Lord. Nevertheless, in comparison to other women in the world, there is so little I have to trust the Lord to provide for me. Daily I do not have to trust the Lord for food, clothes, water, shelter, or transportation. I can provide for myself whatever I want; all I need to do is go and buy them.

The one thing that I am neither able to provide for myself, nor do I want to, is a husband. Whether or not a specific man wants to date me is not entirely up to me. If I am in a relationship with a man, whether he breaks up with me or proposes is not entirely up to me.

I do not want to waste the opportunity that this presents. Singleness is a grand opportunity to trust the Lord, to wait on Him, to seek Him, and to cling to Him. It is also a chance to trust His provision and to not seek to provide for myself. There is a sweetness in singleness because it gives me this chance to fully rely on the Lord. I want to trust my faithful Savior to provide what I need, whether that means I get married or He only gives me more of Himself.

Remember we are all cherished in His sight. Human beings are the crown of His creation. God cares and provides for the birds, and God values people so much more than birds. I do not think we could get to the end of our lives and think we trusted in God's care and provision too much. Wherever we are, whatever we are wrestling with, we need to remember, remember, remember to consider the birds.

JOURNAL QUESTIONS

1. Birds have become a symbol of God's loving care for me. Do you have something in your life that symbolizes God's loving care?
2. When you don't believe God cares about you, how does that impact the way you live?
3. In the past year, how have you trusted in God's care and provision?
4. Write out at least two other verses that remind you of God's care and provision.
5. In moments where you struggle with worry and anxiety, do you remind yourself of these specific verses?

SIX

* * * * * *

Is God Even Good?

The Voice of Christ: *What I have given, I
can take away and restore it when it
pleases Me. What I give remains Mine,
and thus when I take it away I take
nothing that is yours, for every good gift
and every perfect gift is Mine . . . I am no
less just and worthy of great praise when
I deal with you in this way.*

Thomas à Kempis

In our minds, we tend to draw a correlation between what the
Lord has given us and His character. If, when looking at our
lives, it appears we have received the short end of the stick,
then, without knowing it, we can begin to question the goodness of God. I say "without knowing it" because of what I
have seen in my life and in the lives of others. We tend to internalize good circumstances as a reflection of the goodness
of God to us. This leads us to consider trials and hardships as
reasons to question His goodness. Holding up our circumstances as the measurement of the goodness of God is setting
us up to doubt His goodness.

Several years ago, I realized I had set up the areas of my
life—my relationships, jobs, ministries, and health—like

mirrors that reflected how the Lord was treating me. If things were going well, then God was good.

As a trial in one area began to stretch into months, it was as if that mirror was crumbling. When I experienced sudden difficulty in many areas at one time, it was as if multiple mirrors shattered at once. At one point, it felt like God was taking a baseball bat to my mirrors. As a result, I began to have this underlying feeling that God was not being good to me.

It can be easy to look at situations in our lives and think God is not being good to us. Over time, this thought morphs into: "God is not good." This sometimes builds for months without us realizing it, and our hearts grow angry, hard, and bitter. It is in Christianity 101 that we are taught to say, "God is good, all the time." It is the harshness of life that leads us to doubt if that is true.

Singleness can feel hard because we never expected to be single for so long. We thought God would give us the wonderful gift of a spouse. This is often compounded when people on social media talk about their spouses or new babies, especially if they use the taglines: "The Lord has been so good to me" or "God is so good." There is nothing wrong with these taglines, but they feed the nagging thought in the back of my mind that God has not been good to me. God might have good things stored up for others, but not for me.

Sadly, life experiences are often the way we learn the truth of this chapter. Most people will easily agree that God is good. The question is, deep in your heart, will you still believe that when you feel like God has taken a baseball bat to your life? Sometimes it is difficult to determine the underlying emotions in our hearts. We may not realize that we are questioning the goodness of God.

If we can imagine the following conversation between the Lord and us, it can be helpful in gauging our hearts. If the Lord says to us, "Do you believe that I am good?" We will answer with what we were intellectually taught is true. "Yes, Lord, You are good." He asks us again, "Do you believe that I am good?" Again, we reply, "Yes, Lord, You are good." A third time He asks us, "Do you believe that I am good?" Often after going over this question three or four times we, with tears, realize, "No, Lord, I don't think You are good."[1] It is rare for a person to experience difficulty in every area of her life and not question the goodness of God. Those who are in the midst of an extended trial often question His goodness on some level. Most of us, at one point in our lives, came to believe in our hearts that God is good. It is wise to periodically check your heart to see if you still believe that to be true. Disbelief in the goodness of God will kill your desire to follow Him.

Not expecting difficulty or hardship contributes to us doubting God's goodness. Jesus told His disciples, "In this world you will have trouble" (John 16:33). All of us will face various trials throughout our lives. God promises us them, so we should not hold up hardships as evidence that He is not good. Sometimes our mirrors need to shatter, so we can learn to stop looking at them to determine the character of God.

Building our spiritual beliefs is like building a house. Sometimes the sturdiness of what we are building is only determined by going through a storm. For me, I believe that what I am building is solid. It is not my intention to build something incorrectly. The aftermath of a storm exposes structural weaknesses. I have learned not to be too quick to go in and do a patch up job. First, I need to reevaluate the underlying structural issues that contributed to the damage. This might mean tearing down before I can build it back up. If I do not address the underlying issues, then there will be damage again in the same areas after the next storm.

Quick fixes rarely fix anything in the long run. It would be great if Band-Aids were sufficient to heal a gunshot wound. However, if you need surgery or stitches, a Band-Aid is a poor solution. Many people want to move on from trials as quickly as possible, and as a result their hearts never properly heal.

In seasons of my life, I have had to do heart surgery. I have had to relook at how I internalize trials. There were times when I needed to tear down incorrect thoughts. I needed to learn not to measure His goodness based on my circumstances. Sometimes difficulties and hardship are preparation for battles ahead. He does not want us to go into them unprepared. It is a blessing when God helps us see when we are relying on the wrong things. We need to build into our lives an understanding that His goodness is something we can always rely on.

THE HEART OF A FATHER

We need to learn to trust that God is the best Father who gives what is good. "Which of you, if your son asks for bread, will give him a stone? Or if he asks for a fish, will give him a snake? If you, then, though you are evil, know how to give good gifts to your children, how much more will your Father in heaven give good gifts to those who ask him!" (Matt. 7:9–11). Often I whine and complain about not having what I want, rather than trusting God. What is and is not in our lives is the good that God has for us right now. He is not maliciously withholding blessings from us. God is a better and more caring Father than even the best earthly father. If fathers here give nice things to their kids, how much more does your Father in heaven give you good gifts?

Sometimes the gifts we are asking for are not as great as they may seem. It can be a demonstration of a father's protection if he withholds what his child is asking for. If your kid asks for a scorpion, you will exercise your better judgment and not give it to him. What if the "good" thing you desire is not as "good" as it appears?

As adults, it is hard for us to consider that what we are asking for is not in our best interest. We think we know what is best and can usually give a detailed list to support our belief. However, what if you are wrong about what would be good for your life right now? Have you considered that?

If the Lord is not answering our prayers the way we want, this is possibly a demonstration of His goodness to us. Sometimes, after much time has passed, we look back and think, "Praise the Lord that He did not give me what I prayed for." In the moment, though, it is hard to understand why our prayers remain unanswered. There may be times where it seems like He is cruel, but we know Him better; we know that He is good.

He is not cruel, and He gives us many blessings. We are often too busy daydreaming about what we want and do not see the blessings in today. When God gives us temporary and physical blessings, it is right to rejoice over them. Most of us live blessed lives of great material wealth that we take for granted. How often do you miss out on enjoying what you have because you believe the lie that you need one more thing?

We live in the age of comparison and entitlement. As much as we try to avoid these two pitfalls, it is hard to keep them from creeping into our lives. When other people have good things, we compare our lack to their blessing. Our sense of entitlement leads us to think that we should have the same blessing as they do. Our hearts begin to grow hard toward the Lord because it looks like He is withholding good. We use these thoughts to justify either our feelings of resentment or our unrestricted pursuit of what we are lacking. We can get so caught up in pursuing what we think is missing in our lives. We tend to believe we should experience whatever we want to in this world.

It is a deception to think that our life would be better if we just had _____. Our lives would not be better; they would just be different. Life is only found in Jesus, so life is only better as we grow in our relationship with Jesus. Jesus, Himself, is better than all the gifts He gives.

If a father gives his child a birthday present, he would want his kid to feel excited and play with the new toy. The father would not, however, want the child to love the toy more than the child loves him. We should not be like a child more excited over the toys from our Father than spending time with Him. Rather, we should want the Giver of Gifts more than we want the gifts.

When we cherish the gifts over the Giver, it testifies that our focus is on the temporary things of this world. Regardless of our circumstances, we must get to the point where each of us believes not just that God is good in general, but that God has been good *to me*. Even if events in our lives seem to testify that this is not true, we must have a confidence in God's goodness that is independent of our circumstances. Our relationship with God is what we should value more than any of the other things He could give us.

The Good God has Done

God is good, holy, perfect, and righteous. He is all these things, apart from what we may think. Evil in the world is often pointed to as a testament that God must not be good because He allows it in His world. Those who say that are forgetting that God has granted mankind free will. People can choose to sin. Sin causes pain in our lives and the lives of others. Sin is never God's will. Sin is a result of our free will. When we remember free will, evil becomes not a testament against God, but a testimony of the wickedness of humans.

There are hard things that happen outside of human causation. Regardless of the cause of our circumstances, we can rest assured. Even if it looks like evil, feels like evil, smells like evil, God can turn it and use it for good. He specializes in redeeming situations that look irredeemable.

It is rather ironic that human beings so often question the goodness of God. Humans are utterly sinful with hearts inclined to evil. We need to remember this when we start throwing stones at God. If we want to compare something, we should look at who we are in comparison to God. If we maintain a correct perspective, we find ourselves unable to fathom questioning His goodness.

The goodness of God is that He has made a way for this fallen world to be temporary, not permanent. For the Christian, the trials in this life are the worst we will ever have to endure. There is pain in this life when God's will is not done on earth as it is in heaven. The goodness of God is that He has made a way for us to go to heaven. He did not have to come for us. He could have left us drowning in our sin. Instead, "He has rescued us from the dominion of darkness and brought us into the kingdom of the Son he loves, in whom we have redemption, the forgiveness of sins" (Col. 1:13–14).

It is no small thing to have my sins forgiven by a holy God, and even more than that I have been given His righteousness. I have never laid eyes on another person who has thought and done everything right. Jesus was the only one who accomplished that. The good news is that because Jesus died for my sins when I placed my faith and trust in Him our records were swapped. He took the punishment that my long list of sins deserved, and He gave me His righteousness. When God looks at me He does not see all the ways I have messed up. He sees Jesus's righteousness—as if I had thought and done everything right. "This righteousness is given through faith in Jesus Christ to all who believe" (Rom. 3:22). It is easy for me to believe that God is good when I remember what He has done for me.

The Lord has blessed me in so many ways. He has brought me into a relationship with Him, forgiven me, revealed Himself to me, allowed me to know His Word, redeemed me, made me new, cleansed me of all my sin, and given me His righteousness. This is obviously an incomplete list of the good things that God has done for me in Christ. As a child who tires of my toys, I overlook and take for granted what my good Father has given me. When did the good news stop being enough for me to believe in the goodness of God?

In a way, my questioning of the goodness of God reveals that I undervalue the presence of God. "You are my Lord; apart from you I have no good thing" (Ps. 16:2). Apart from the Lord I have no good thing, and if I get nothing else, I already have what is best.

One time last year after contemplating this verse, I went on my usual prayer walk on the trail through the woods. On that walk I realized: the highest demonstration of God's goodness to me is that He would let me be in His presence.

If I am honest, my flesh thinks His goodness to me would be for Him to fulfill all my desires now. Waiting for a while is fine, but then my patience wears thin. I am deceived into thinking the gifts will satisfy more than the Giver. My only hope is to preach to my own heart what is true. Apart from him, I have no good thing. Seeing my desire for marriage fulfilled is not His greatest gift. The best demonstration of His goodness to me is His presence.

His goodness to us is not measured in favorable circumstances. It is not measured in Him giving us everything we want, like an overindulgent parent. It is not measured by whether He works things out for me to get married in my time frame. There is nothing in all existence that God could give or grant us that would be better than His presence. If we correctly value the presence of God, then we will rejoice in His presence, not question His goodness. There is not a better treasure that He could give you.

If we get good gifts in this life, we should be thankful, but we should never cherish the gifts more than the Giver. If we do not get the good gifts we want, we should still be thankful because God made a way for us to be with Him forever. Life is hard, but God is good, and heaven will be great; do not lose sight of the last two in the midst of the first.

JOURNAL QUESTIONS

1. In what ways do you struggle to enjoy what you have because you think you need one more thing?
2. How are your current circumstances a demonstration of the goodness of God?
3. How does Jesus's death on the cross reveal that God is good?
4. On a scale of 0–10, how much do you value the presence of God? And why?
5. Write out two other verses that remind you of the goodness of God and reflect on why they remind you of His goodness.

SEVEN

* * * * * *

DOES GOD NOT LOVE ME?

Could we with ink the ocean fill,
And were the skies of parchment made;
Were every stalk on earth a quill,
And every man a scribe by trade.
To write the love of God above,
Would drain the ocean dry;
Nor could the scroll contain the whole,
Though stretched from sky to sky.

Unknown[1]

One question many nonbelievers have is if God is a loving God, how can there be so much pain in this world? When we find ourselves going through a difficult trial, we often ask a similar question: If God loves me, how can He allow so much pain and heartache in my life? If we doubt God's love, it will be hard for us to trust Him.

In horrible situations, some people say that things can only get better; they can't get any worse. I have been in many bad situations that have only grown worse. My motto is: "no matter how bad things are, they can always get worse." If I am only looking at what is going on in these situations, it is hard to be confident that God loves me.

In our culture, if someone says they love us we expect them to show it in what they do and how they treat us. The way we often measure someone's love for us is by their actions and their words. If we ask someone to do something for us but they do not do it, then we begin to question if they truly love us. It is also hard for us to trust their love if we feel that they are treating us in a way that is harsh and unjust.

We often carry over this attitude into how we view the Lord. If we continue praying for something but nothing changes, we question if He loves us. Difficult circumstances that appear harsh or unjust to us seem to testify that He does not love us. A prolonged unfulfilled desire for marriage plants doubts in the back of our minds. We can think: *If the Lord loved me, surely my circumstances would have changed already! I would not be single right now—if the Lord's heart were for me.*

We rarely consider that our trials could be a blessing from the Lord. My singleness may be a demonstration of God's love for me. In my twisted thinking, it would be an act of God's love for me if a certain man asked me out. However, that is a narrow view. It could be a demonstration of God's love for me to remain single. There are days where I recognize that, out of love, He might be sparing me the difficulty and pain that comes with marriage. But other days I can be like a child whining that if God loves me, He would give me what I want.

If we are going to try to measure the love of God, we should not simply look at the pain and heartache in our lives or this world. We must factor in how He has demonstrated His love in light of eternity. We must look at all His actions and words, and not only at what we experience today.

It is because of God's love for us that He forgives us. He did not send Jesus because He was apathetic or bored.

Rather, God's great love for us compelled Him to be planning, plotting, and orchestrating from the beginning a way for us to spend an eternity with Him.

If we ever doubt God's love, all we need to do is look to the cross. The cross will always represent the greatest demonstration of the love of God.

People generally fall into two categories. Either they struggle with believing God loves them because they feel they are so unworthy, or they struggle to recognize their sin and their need for a Savior. Sometimes people flip-flop back and forth between the two.

All Need a Savior

People who have trouble seeing their sin and their need for a Savior are usually comparing themselves to others rather than the standard of God. Some do not actually know God's standard for holy and perfect living. They do not recognize their disobedience of the commands of God because they do not know the commands of God. No one in their right mind would declare themselves innocent of lying, jealousy, greed, gossip, lust, arrogance, selfish ambition, stealing, fits of rage, hatred, drunkenness, deceit, slander, and impurity (Col. 3:5–9; Gal. 5:19–21; Mark 7:21–29; Rom. 1:29–32). Some may claim they have not done *all* of those things, therefore they are still good enough to get into heaven. They forget that Adam and Eve could not remain in Eden because they had committed *one* sin.

Every act of disobedience, every lie, every lustful look, every word spoken in malice, and every moment of pride is stacked against us. The truth is not that there are plenty of good people who deserve to go to heaven. The truth is no one deserves to go to heaven. No one is good enough to stand before a holy, perfect, righteous God and tell Him that they deserve to go to heaven.

Jesus even posed a question to the religious leaders in His day. They thought they were too good to be in the same category with sinners. "How will you escape being condemned to hell?" (Matt. 23:33).

It is because of love that Jesus died the death that we deserve. In His death, He took the penalty, the punishment, and the wrath we deserve upon Himself. Love is what motivated God to send Jesus to pay for our sins so that we could have a relationship with Him.

ALL UNWORTHY

Many Christians wrestle with feeling unworthy of the love of God. They constantly turn over in their minds the idea that God can't possibly love them.

There is a lot written in the world today trying to help people feel a greater sense of self-worth. For many Christians, this is a hard issue because they see their sins, their failures, their shortcomings, their doubts, their fears, and their weaknesses as signs of being unworthy. In light of the ways they fall short, it is hard to feel worthy. They find themselves continuously plagued by doubts of God's love. The problem is we often look at this wrong. We forget the central message of the gospel: because we are all unworthy, we all need a Savior.

Every human being has worth and value because God made us in His image. You have worth, but that does not mean you are worthy of the Lord. The central message of the gospel is that, in and of yourself, you do not deserve to go to heaven. According to the Bible, you are unworthy of standing in the presence of God. The gospel is not that you are such a great and wonderful person that you deserve the love, kindness, mercy, affection, blessing, and forgiveness of God. It is the opposite.

You are unworthy and do not deserve the grace of God. No one does. Grace is the unmerited favor of God. Our innate sense of unworthiness is meant to drive us humbly to the foot of the cross. The gospel is not that we scrape together everything in our lives that testifies that we are worthy and hold it out to God in order for Him to accept us. Rather it is: scrape it all together, multiply by 100, weigh it on a scale, and you will still be found wanting. Even the best of everyone's efforts combined would still be undeserving of the love and grace of God.

The core of the gospel is not that you measure up; it is that *you do not* measure up. One of the first few verses many of us learn is "for all have sinned and fall short of the glory of God" (Rom. 3:23). We should all feel we have fallen short. Many wrestle with feeling that we have fallen short and are unworthy of the love of God—as if that is a problem. The problem is that you have not fully embraced the truth that God loves you anyway.

Subconsciously you may think you have to do something to try to earn it. Then, when you continue to fall short, you feel overwhelmed by your sense of unworthiness. The solution to feeling unworthy will never be to try harder, do better, or work more, but to embrace that God loves you anyway.

If you feel you are worthy of the love of God, then that makes you a proud Pharisee. In Luke, we have the example of what Jesus said to those who thought they were worthy.

To some who were confident of their own righteousness and looked down on everyone else, Jesus told this parable: "Two men went up to the temple to pray, one a Pharisee and the other a tax collector. The Pharisee stood by himself and prayed: 'God, I thank you that I am not like other people—robbers, evildoers, adulterers—or even like this tax collector. I fast twice a week and give a tenth of all I get.' But the tax collector stood at a distance. He would not even look up to heaven, but beat his breast and said, 'God, have mercy on me, a sinner.' I tell you that this man, rather than the other, went home justified before God." (Luke 18:9–14)

It is necessary that we recognize that we are sinners in need of mercy. Self-confidence in our own righteousness is always a stumbling block in our relationship with Jesus.

Somehow as Christians, we have bought into the cultural idea that we all need to have a greater sense of self-worth, but we wonder why it is so difficult. We fail to see that recognizing our own unworthiness is crucial to becoming a Christian.

Isaiah stood in the presence of God and cried, "Woe is me," because he stood there and found the only thing he was worthy of was death (Isa. 6:5). Jesus did not die on the cross because you were already worthy of being in the presence of God. He died to deal with everything that makes you unworthy.

Gomer's sense of worth was not found in being a prostitute, but in being the bride of Hosea the prophet. Israel's sense of worth was not found in their obedience or lack thereof, but in being the chosen people of God. We should not look to ourselves for a greater sense of self-worth because we will always come up deficient. That is the way it should be in light of the gospel. We should find our sense of self-worth in being the bride of Christ, the people of God, and the redeemed of the Lord.

We have worth because He graciously bought us with His blood. The cross will always stand as testimony to the love of God for a people who do not deserve it. Jesus's death on the cross was the most unjust moment in history: a perfectly innocent man dying a sinner's death, taking the wrath of God that we deserved.

The love of God will never motivate us to serve Him for the long haul if we think we deserve His love. It is not that we are worthy; it is that He is worthy. To the degree that we grasp and accept the love of God despite all our failures, to that same degree we will praise, worship, and serve Him with our lives.

The life of the sinful woman demonstrates this concept.

> A woman in that town who lived a sinful
> life learned that Jesus was eating at the
> Pharisee's house, so she came there with
> an alabaster jar of perfume. As she stood
> behind him at his feet weeping, she began
> to wet his feet with her tears. Then she
> wiped them with her hair, kissed them and
> poured perfume on them. . . . Jesus said . . .

> "I tell you, her many sins have been for-
> given—as her great love has shown. But
> whoever has been forgiven little loves
> little." (Luke 7:37–38, 47)

If we understand the love and grace of God her response is not radical. Would you honor Jesus in a similar way? Balking at the thought can be an indicator that you do not grasp either your deep need for forgiveness or the depth to which God through Jesus forgives you.

I would like to add that some people wrestle with feeling worthless far more than they should. This is often a result of mental, emotional, physical, or sexual abuse experienced during childhood. The result is that they feel utterly unworthy of anyone's love, including parents, spouse, children, and friends. Believing God really loves you is very difficult if you do not believe that anyone could ever love you. Often you will need to address these deeper wounds in order for them to heal and for you to believe in the core of your being that anyone loves you. Please seek help in processing these wounds, so you can fully embrace the love of God and others. The Lord did not make His love known to you so that you would always be second guessing it, but instead so that you could be confident in it.

DESIRE FOR LOVE

There could never be a greater demonstration of love than the cross of Calvary. If we grasp what happened on that cross, we would never be able to look at the cross and doubt the love of God. Keeping my eyes fixed on Jesus and what He has done for me gives me a greater confidence in God's love.

If only I could always remain confident in the sufficiency of the love of the Lord. I am often weary of the fickleness of my heart. One minute I am cherishing the love of God and holding onto it because it is my life. The next minute I am questioning it or wanting to exchange it for someone more tangible.

Let us not be deceived: the love of a man will never satisfy our hearts. Human love does not satisfy the longing of the heart; it was never meant to and it never will. We can never have enough love. Even if a human were capable of giving us all the love that their heart, mind, soul, body could produce, it would not satisfy our longing for love. We will never get to the point where we will say, "I have had enough love for this lifetime." We all get to the point where we have had enough pain and heartache for this lifetime, but we never get to the point of having enough genuine, sincere love.

Our unsatisfiable desire for love is meant to point us to the love of God. The love of the Lord has no end, no limit. It is steadfast, unconditional, and unfailing. It will never be less than what you hope for—it will always be better. It is only His love that satisfies our hearts. Our desire for love was not designed to be satisfied by anything this world can offer; it was meant to point us to the Source of Love outside of what we see.

If this world is all there is, then there is no reason we would have an unsatisfiable desire for love. If this world is all there is, almost anyone would meet our desire for love. Almost anyone can meet a desire for physical pleasure, but our desire for genuine love is not so easily met.

The love of God is greater than our hearts currently have the capacity to experience. In this life, we only get a taste of

God's love. We will experience the overwhelming fullness of His love when we see Him face-to-face in heaven. His love surpasses what we are capable of wrapping our minds around; it surpasses knowledge. There is a depth to the love of God we will not fully grasp until we get to heaven. However, if we grasped the height, width, depth, and breadth of the love of God that He has revealed to us—which we are able to understand—it would transform our lives and satisfy our souls.

Singleness is not God trying to tell us that He thinks we are unworthy of being someone's wife. We are the bride of Christ. If no one else wants to marry you, rest assured the Lord always wants you as His bride. Some people seek a spouse in an attempt to heal their feelings of unworthiness by assuaging their heart that someone finds them worthy.

An unshakeable sense of self-worth is never found in acceptance by another human because their acceptance of us can always change. It is only found in the cross, based on the price that God has paid for us. We have value because an object is worth what you pay for it. Jesus paid a great price to redeem us, so we have great value. We now belong to God forever.

His love for you is beyond measure, which is why He was willing to sacrifice His Son for you. In relationships, people are often seeking to feel loved. Marriage should not be about feeling more loved than you already are—that is not possible. Only God knows you completely and loves you completely. No spouse's love will ever compare to the love of God.

Every day we should spend time remembering, cherishing, enjoying, and basking in His love. It is impossible to meditate on the love of God too much. The Bible is full of countless verses telling us of the Lord's love for us. I encourage you to pick out several of them and review them regularly. Truly understanding the love of God will blow our minds. Grasping the depth to which we do not deserve it will make us fall on our faces. Accepting the fact that it has been freely bestowed on us will transform our lives.

Our struggle with sin throughout our lives will always attest to our unworthiness of the Lord's unfailing love. Even when we are the worst of sinners, His love never changes. Love He demonstrated in blood, in sweat, and in tears. May our hearts always be undone by the steadfast love of the Lord. No matter how many years I have been following the Lord, I never want to get to the point where what happened on the cross becomes passé. Whatever gut-wrenching trials the Lord allows in my life, the cross forever remains the greatest demonstration of the love of God.

I should not measure His love for me by the temporary blessings in my life. If my circumstances only go from bad to worse, it is not a sign that His love for me has failed. I can always look to the cross to remind me that the Lord's love for me endures forever.

JOURNAL QUESTIONS

1. In what ways do you struggle with seeing your need for a Savior?

2. In what ways do you struggle with either believing God loves you or feeling unworthy?

3. How does Jesus's death on the cross demonstrate God's love for you?

4. Do you think God deserves your praise, worship, and service? Why?

5. If you want to get married, why do you want to get married?

6. How does God meet your emotional needs?

EIGHT

* * * * * *

WHAT IS MY PURPOSE?

Dare to have it out with God, and ask Him to
show you whether or not all is focused on
Christ and His Glory. Turn your soul's vision
to Jesus, and look and look at Him, and a
strange dimness will come over all that is
apart from Him.

Lilias Trotter

If we love someone, the real focus is not on our selfish gain. Our focus is not on what we can get from them. Our focus is on what we can give them. As we reflect on how we can show and demonstrate our love for the Lord, we need to consider how He wants us to express it. We think we know best what we should do, but we need to consider what the Lord has for us to do.

A few years ago, I was sitting in church listening to a sermon when the pastor quoted from Colossians 1:16: "All things have been created through him and for him." He emphasized the last two words: *for Him*. His point was that we should consider why God made us. We often live as if we have been created for our own purposes, but God created us for Him, for His purposes. It was a very small part of the sermon. The pastor moved on with the rest of it, but my thoughts did not move on.

My mind was stuck on that simple concept. God created us for Him, not for ourselves. Likewise, God redeemed us for Him, to use us for His intended purposes. In recognizing this, we should seek to align ourselves under His overall mission. Our focus too often is on ourselves and on how we want to spend our time.

We sometimes get things backward. We tend to think God exists to fulfill the desires of our hearts and make our dreams come true. Whatever we think is best for our lives, He is under an obligation to make it happen, right? As if He is our own personal genie, who will grant our wishes. In our warped thinking, we can think that He should do whatever we ask like a slave.

As I sat there that day in church, my thoughts were also drawn to how this applied to my life in singleness. I think I know what would be the best plan for my life, that I would get married and have a family. In those moments, the focus of my heart is on my own plans, as if fulfillment is found in them. I lose sight of the truth that I was created by Him, for Him. Before that day, I had never given much thought to what that verse in Colossians meant. Since God created me for Himself, I should think more about living for Him and for His purposes.

As I was reading through the Bible this year, I noticed another verse that said the same thing. I have read this verse many times, but before that sermon, this part had never stuck out to me. "There is but one God, the Father, from whom are all things and we exist for Him" (1 Cor. 8:6 NASB). The end is what grabbed my attention. We exist for Him. Think about what that means, what that implies.

Fulfillment does not come from within us or from perfect

circumstances. Our lives are so full of selfish pursuits. We spend so much of our time, energy, and money doing what we want to do, how we want to do it, and when we want to do it. In the end, we still come up empty. Selfish pursuits always leave us wanting more because we were not created to find fulfillment in them. The implications of being created for Him and existing for Him include that we will find fulfillment in Him, in living for Him, and in accomplishing His purposes for our lives.

IT'S ABOUT A RELATIONSHIP

We were made to be in an intimate relationship with God. There is nothing more important than our relationship with Him. In it, we find everything we want. Without it, no matter what else we obtain, we will still feel something is missing.

If we are not deeply abiding with God, we are missing out. "For in him we live and move and have our being" (Acts 17:28). Of course, Christians have the Holy Spirit, so He is always with us. However, our hearts and minds can be so focused on other things that we miss out on deeply connecting with Him. I love the imagery of drawing up a chair next to Him, sitting at His feet, or going on a walk with Him. In the New Testament, it says, "Draw near to God and He will draw near to you" (James 4:8 NASB). While all Christians have the Spirit, there is an intimacy with the Lord that we can choose to grow and cultivate.

If we grasp that we exist for Him, it will impact what we pursue. There are so many things we can seek, but time is limited. We always have time for what is important to us. "God looks down from heaven on all mankind to see if there are any who understand, any who seek God" (Ps. 53:2). The problem is we do not understand the rich depth of a relationship that we can have with God right now. Even the most mature among us understand only a fraction of the depth. We do not understand, so instead we seek comfort and pleasure. Even Christians who were once living for God can slide into living for their own comfort and pleasure.

LIVE FOR CHRIST

There are many verses that point to the idea of not living for ourselves but living for His purposes. "And he died for all, that those who live should no longer live for themselves but for him who died for them and was raised again" (2 Cor. 5:15). Those who know Christ should no longer live for themselves, but they should live for Him.

It is easy to lose sight of this because our entire world seems to be screaming the opposite. The culture is all about living for yourself and pursuing whatever makes you feel good. But the Christian is to live for Christ, to do whatever He wants them to do, and to pursue what is pleasing to the Lord.

There are bigger fish to fry than whether my plans for marriage are fulfilled the way I want. It is not that other people are more important or valuable to Him than me. He has a bigger plan He is unfolding, a bigger mission He is accomplishing, a bigger kingdom that He is building. Whether married or single, I know God wants me to be involved in His purposes, in advancing His kingdom.

There is a tendency to live for myself that I need to crucify. "I have been crucified with Christ and I no longer live, but Christ lives in me. The life I now live in the body, I live by faith in the Son of God, who loved me and gave himself for me" (Gal. 2:20). I have been thinking about what it means to live a crucified life, to live a life dedicated to Him, to live yielded to His will. The overarching focus of my life should not be living for the fulfillment of my own personal desires. I hope you see how self-focused we are, how wrapped up in ourselves we tend to live, rather than the Christ-centered, gospel-focused lives He calls us to live.

God redeems people, and He redeems them for a purpose. "But you are a chosen race, a royal priesthood, a holy nation, a people for God's own possession, so that you may proclaim the excellencies of Him who has called you out of darkness into His marvelous light" (1 Pet. 2:9 NASB). We are all these things for a reason. The 'so that' means that there is something more than just being those things, and that is to proclaim Him. He called us out of darkness so that we would praise Him and make known what He has done for us.

SERVE HIS PURPOSES

Our greatest need is to have our sins forgiven and our relationship with God restored. That is everyone's greatest need. God wants us to join Him in accomplishing His plan of seeing people come to know Him. In another verse it says:

> God, who reconciled us to himself through Christ and gave us the ministry of reconciliation: that God was reconciling the world to himself in Christ, not counting people's sins against them. And He has committed to us the message of reconciliation. We are therefore Christ's ambassadors, as though God were making His appeal through us.

> We implore you on Christ's behalf: Be
> reconciled to God. (2 Cor. 5:18–20)

He has given us the ministry of reconciliation. If God is going to make His appeal through us, we have to be willing to open our mouths. Jesus is not here still sharing the gospel. Instead, He has left you here to share the gospel. Jesus said, "I will remain in the world no longer, but they are still in the world" (John 17:11). We are still in this world to represent Him and to serve His purposes by loving people and speaking truth.

Consider your life. Your days are numbered, as well as the days of every person you see. Two hundred years from now, no one you know will still be alive. If we live only for ourselves, we have no concern for the salvation of others. If we live for God, we begin more and more to see people from His perspective. We begin to think about how we can impact and influence people's lives for Christ.

"Live as free people, but do not use your freedom as a cover-up for evil; live as God's slaves" (1 Pet. 2:16). How often do you use your freedom in Christ as a cover-up instead of actually living as a slave of God? Hopefully you do not use it as a cover-up for evil or wickedness. But how often do you use your freedom in Christ as a cover-up for complacency or a cover-up for pursuing your own desires? We have all spent too much time doing everything other than living as slaves of God.

LOVE UNIQUELY

Consider how the Lord has made you and consider your life experiences. The Lord has made each of us look physically unique, and I think there is a purpose in this as well. If you looked different, then your childhood, teenage, and college experience would have been different. Our life experiences—the good, bad, and ugly—shape and impact us in unique ways. This makes each of us individually suited for advancing God's kingdom in different ways. We all exist for Him, but there are unique ways that He wants to use each of us. God never intended for us to look identical, and He never intended to use us in identical ways.

Advancing God's kingdom can take a variety of shapes, sizes, and forms. As we look for some bigger way to impact the world, we can overlook the people in our lives. Some of us may get to do crazy big things that impact a multitude of lives, and some of us may only impact the life of one. We often want to feel as if we are accomplishing something big and meaningful with our lives. This causes us wrestle with the insignificance of our day-to-day lives. Huge world-changing things are not what God has for most of us. Instead, He is asking us to faithfully love Him and the people around us.

Loving the people right in front of us is the bigger way God wants to use us. God cares about and values each person. Loving one person is significant to God. Sometimes the bigger thing God has for us is to embrace the simple life of loving God and loving people. To Him, that is big stuff.

Loving people is sometimes painful. Sometimes you get burned. God is asking you to genuinely love people anyway. Love people and trust Him to heal our hearts when others hurt us. A self-protecting bubble is not what God has called us to build. Whatever happens, He is always more than able to restore my soul, revive my heart, refresh my spirit, and renew my strength. I only need to turn to Him.

DIFFICULT SEASONS

At times, we have seasons where the Lord is leading us beside quiet waters, and it feels boring and mundane. We do not always see His purpose in these times until we are in the chaos of intense raging rapids. I love adventure and challenges. Too often I long for the rapids when the Lord gives me a quiet stream. Over the years, I have learned to be content in the quiet seasons knowing from experience the tough ones will come eventually. Whether crazy and intense or boring and mundane, whatever the Lord wants me to do with my life, I want to do it.

If your attitude is that the Lord can do whatever He wants with your life, you do not get to exclude difficulty.

> This is the word that came to Jeremiah from the Lord: "Go down to the potter's house, and there I will give you my message.". . . Then the word of the Lord came to me. He said, "Can I not do with you, Israel, as this potter does?". . . This is what the Lord says: "Go and buy a clay jar from a potter . . . Then break the jar." (Jer. 18:1-2, 5–6; 19:1, 10)

Being surrendered to the Lord's purposes includes letting Him make me into a beautiful clay jar, only then to break me. He is not illogical, but He has a purpose behind how He makes us. If He breaks us, there will be a purpose to that as well. He is looking for people who will give their lives to Him without limitations or expectations.

Looking back, when I first became a Christian and started

following the Lord, I had no idea what I was signing up for. I take comfort that the disciples did not get it at first either. They had a huge fight over which of them was the greatest because they were focusing on themselves. Eventually, these men would realize following Jesus was not about their exaltation or greatness. They would see that they were being called to follow in His footsteps, to lay down their lives for His kingdom, to deny themselves, to go where they did not want to go, to crucify their desires, to take up their cross, and to submit their will to His. As it was with them, so it is with us. I often pray that I would be willing to accept whatever the Lord has for my life, even if it is not what I want.

Ultimately, the Lord created you for Himself, and you will always find the greatest fulfillment in Him. Fulfillment is in knowing Him, walking with Him, and living for Him because that is why you exist. As you go through life, I pray you will always remember that God created you for Him and for His purposes.

JOURNAL QUESTIONS

1. What is the focus and purpose of your life (regardless of your current season or circumstances)?
2. Do you have a specific focus and purpose that is related to your current season of life? What is it?
3. In the past how have you been hurt by loving people?
4. On a scale of 0–10, how willing are you to except whatever the Lord has your life—even when it's not what you want? Why did you pick that number?

NINE

* * * * * *

WHAT AM I DOING WITH MY LIFE?

*I have served Satan much in my
younger years, and I desire now with
all my might to serve God, during the
remaining days of my earthly
pilgrimage. Every day decreases the
number of days that I have to stay on
earth. I therefore desire with all my
might to work.*

George Müller

In singleness, there is a lot of freedom. We decide how we
invest or waste our time. We decide how we spend our
money. We decide what we expend our energy on. What are
you doing with your time, money, and energy? Do you use
your freedom to feed your flesh or to serve God and others?

In my life, it was important for me to realize that before I
was a Christian I was spiritually dead. "You were dead in
your transgressions and sins . . . But because of his great love
for us, God, who is rich in mercy, made us alive with Christ"
(Eph. 2:1, 4–5). I was dead in my sin, but God raised me up
from the dead and gave me life. There are two ways that
Jesus raised my life up from the dead. One is obvious; He
saved me from being dead in my sin and condemned to an
eternal death in hell. Secondly, He raised me up from the

dead and empty way of living. He saved me from wasting my life on myself.

There is much in life that is empty and vain, but there is no greater vanity than spending all of your life on selfish pursuits. Before I became a Christian and started following Jesus, my life was about me. It revolved around me. I did what I wanted to do when I wanted to do it. My focus was on building my own comfortable kingdom.

In following Jesus, there is a paradigm shift. My life is about Jesus, and it revolves around Him. My heart is to do what He wants me to do when He wants me to do it. His kingdom is the kingdom I seek to build, even at great cost to my personal comfort and convenience.

At times building His kingdom has cost me, but it is humbling to think about how much of my life is still all about me.

In singleness, my default tends to be thinking of myself too much. Too often I make decisions based on what is comfortable, convenient, beneficial, and pleasurable to me. The Lord redeemed me, so I should live differently than those that do not know Him. "You were redeemed from the empty way of life handed down to you from your ancestors" (1 Pet. 1:18).

I should base my decisions on different criteria. The focus should be on if it is beneficial to His kingdom. Even if it is uncomfortable, inconvenient, disadvantageous, and unpleasant, these should not be the deciding factors. When I get off track in the Christian life, it is usually because I am focusing too much on my selfish desires. To spend our lives serving God and others requires that we die to ourselves. We will never go the extra mile in serving if our focus is on what is a blessing to us.

MIXED MOTIVES

Our motive for serving God and others needs to be grounded and rooted in the gospel. Both our love and service needs to flow out of our understanding that God has proven His love for us on the cross. "We love because he first loved us" (1 John 4:19). If the motive for our love and labor is some other reason, then our motives are off.

Burnout usually happens for one of two reasons: either we are not resting, or our motivations are off. Even when our motivations are right, we are not machines. We need to rest in the Lord and feed our souls.

Many different motivations can prompt our service. When we do things for the wrong reason, we grow weary faster. The most common wrong motive is the praise and approval of other people. This means you serve because you want pastors, leaders, or other people to notice you. You want others to think well of you and acknowledge what you have done. This leads to discouragement and bitterness when you do not get the recognition you think you deserve. We should be willing to serve even when no one sees it.

If you are trying to earn the favor of God, then you will become bitter towards Him when He does not give you what you think you deserve. The reverse can also be true. We can think we do not deserve a hard trial in our lives because we have been serving the Lord for so many years. The motive for our service should not be earning an easy, blessed life.

God does not owe you anything. He does not owe you a husband, a job promotion, a successful ministry, a baby, or a healthy body. Be on guard against assuming that you will serve God and that, in return, He is obligated to do something. You owe Him everything, not the other way around.

Another false motivation for service is seeking our own approval. This means we serve God and others simply so we will approve of ourselves and feel good about ourselves. There are many good works done by Christians in order for them to feel better about themselves. We would feel bad if we did not serve, so we do it to ensure that we approve of ourselves.

Most people's actions are usually prompted by a combination of right and wrong motives. Sometimes when we see our motives are wrong we can react by thinking we should stop whatever we are doing. There may be times when people need to step back from ministry, but this is not usually the case. If we wait until our motives are pure, we may never do anything.

In the New Testament, Paul addressed an issue where people's motives were off. In Philippi, rivalry and envy motivated Christians to preach the gospel. Paul responded by writing: "The important thing is that in every way, whether from false motives or true, Christ is preached" (Phil. 1:18). Paul did not say stop building God's kingdom until all your actions rise from pure motives. In the same way, we do not need to stop serving until we get all our motives sorted out. We should examine our reasons for why we serve, and we should seek to have gospel-centered motives. However, we should continue serving as we work through our motives.

Figuring out our motivations can be messy. We may never be free of all false motives, but we burnout faster when they are off. Those who continue to serve the Lord for the rest of their lives are usually motived by God's heart for them and others. Our service should flow out an appreciation for God's love and all He has done for us.

ONE OPINION, ONE LIFE

Apart from our motives, there are two main reasons that people do not serve. It either boils down to selfishness or fear. If someone asks me to serve in some area at the last minute, it is usually selfishness that makes me decline. I had a date planned with a cup of tea, a blanket, and a book. If someone is asking me to serve in an area that is new to me, it is usually fears that hold me back. Sometimes a fear that I have no idea what I am doing and will probably mess it up.

For many years I had a fear that people would see me serving and think I was only doing it so they would notice me. If there was going to be an audience or a witness to my acts of service, then I would avoid doing it like it was the plague. I was afraid people would think I wanted them to be aware of the ways I was serving.

Fear of the opinions of others will always hold you back and suffocate you. Eventually, I decided if people saw me serving and misjudged my motives, it did not matter. The Lord knew I was not serving to be seen, and that was good enough for me. I had become secure enough in the Lord's opinion of me that I cared less about people's opinion of me.

We need to get our motives right, die to ourselves, conquer our fears, and serve sacrificially. You only have one life. If someone gives you $50,000 you only get to decide how to spend that money once. You can invest it or spend it frivolously. When it is gone, it is gone. Our lives are the same way. God has given you one life; you only get to spend it once.

There is a limited number of things we can do in a week or a weekend. We chose how we spend our time. I want my life to show that Jesus and His kingdom are the clear winners in my list of priorities. When other people see my life, I want them to see that I believe it is worth it to follow Jesus. If someone were to look at your life, what would they see are your priorities? Do the pleasures and recreations of this world have a decreasing or increasing hold on your heart?

JESUS IS THE EXAMPLE

When it comes to serving, Jesus is always our example. "The Son of Man did not come to be served, but to serve" (Matt. 20:28). If anyone had the right to be served instead of serving, it was Jesus, but he came to serve. Jesus taught His disciples to follow in His ways. "The student is not above the teacher, but everyone who is fully trained will be like their teacher" (Luke 6:40). When we are fully trained in following Jesus, we will live the way He lived. Do you desire to be like Jesus in your serving?

This past year, this verse convicted me: "Whoever claims to live in him must live as Jesus did" (1 John 2:6). *Must live as Jesus did?* Please tell me I read that wrong. The implications of this verse encompass our entire lives. Living as Jesus lived includes loving as Jesus loved and serving as Jesus served. Sometimes I wonder if I am even trying.

There is a depth to the servanthood of Jesus that I have not yet fully grasped. He is God, in the flesh, serving His creation. The human race serving the Creator of the universe makes sense. His coming to serve us—there are no words.

Jesus humbling Himself to serve selflessly is the example we are to follow. In light of what He has done for us, how can we not serve Him? How can we spend our lives on mere selfish pursuits?

We serve Him by loving and serving others. Everywhere

you look, people have needs. There are endless opportunities to serve and ways to show kindness. If God's love demonstrated on the cross motivates us, then even our service is an act of worship.

VOLUNTEER TO SERVE

Many people do not easily see needs or opportunities to serve. I guarantee that if you ask your church leaders, they will give you a list of things to choose from. There is the famous 80/20 rule. In most churches, 20 percent of the people do 80 percent of the work and give 80 percent of the financial support. The bulk of the church, the 80 percent, does barely 20 percent of the work. Do not be a part of the 80 percent of the church that volunteers to help with practically nothing.

If you have been serving in an area for several years, it is okay if you do not want to continue doing a specific ministry forever. Others may rise to the occasion if they see there is a need, but will not do so if you continue to fill the role. One of the best ways to not leave a void is to find your own replacement.

As singles, we have a capacity to serve outside the home that moms do not always have. The more kids you have, the harder it is to wrangle them all in and take them with you as you serve. There are mothers who get their kids to church long before the service starts so they can help with greeting, nursery, or Sunday school. This is a great way to teach kids to serve, but not every family has this capacity.

When you are single, you have more freedom to choose to help lead and serve in many different ministries. One of the great things about singleness is that you control your schedule. However, your life is not your own: you were bought with a price and you should seek to live your life in a way that is worthy of the gospel of Christ (1 Cor. 6:19–20; Phil. 1:27). Do not spend your life selfishly doing what you want to do. Seek the kingdom of God and seek to be a blessing to the church.

My first opportunity to serve came my sophomore year of college when someone asked me to teach Sunday school. This class had about ten elementary age students. It was torture, and I constantly looked at the clock to see how much time remained. I had zero classroom management skills. It frustrated me that I could not figure out how to get them to pay attention.

After several Sundays, one of the pastors asked me how I liked teaching Sunday school? I did not want to lie, so I may or may not have used the term cruel and unusual punishment. My heart was to serve anywhere that there was a need, so I was still willing to continue teaching. However, this pastor declined my offer to continue helping, and I have not taught Sunday school since.

Helping with vacation Bible school every year reconfirms my feelings on this area. For one week they need all the help they can get, so I volunteer to assist in a classroom. By the end of the first night, I have reaffirmed that this is not my cup of tea.

Teaching Sunday school might not be my thing, but there are many other opportunities to serve. There is always a need for volunteers in the nursery on Sunday. Since it takes no skill beyond making sure kids do not throw things at one another, I can handle that. I can even make it through without too many glances at the clock.

It is always great to serve where we know we will like what we are doing. Often, though, there is a gap between need and people who are willing to help at all. We need to be willing to stand in the gap, even if that means teaching Sunday school for a season. You can try out different areas, and you might actually find out that you like serving in that area. If you do not, remember you do not have to keep serving in that area forever.

The year after I graduated from college, my church was looking for volunteers to help with middle school ministry. If you would have asked me, "Do you feel qualified to help with middle school ministry?" I would have responded, "No, I have no idea how to relate to a middle schooler, how to interact with a middle schooler, what to talk to them about, or how to teach at their level." I volunteered anyway. This was partially due to the fact that I had a thirteen-year-old sister. I wanted to learn all these things in order to reach out to her.

Over the years I have learned a lot, but there have been moments where I felt just as awkward as the middle schoolers. When the middle schoolers went on to high school, I transitioned to high school ministry. Later, the ministry structure changed into a 7th–12th grade teen ministry. Thankfully teen ministry has worked out much better for me than Sunday school. I have really enjoyed it. The original group of middle school girls is now in college, and it has been a blessing to see them grow in their relationships with Christ.

MAKE SACRIFICES NOT EXCUSES

Sometimes we will not know whether we like serving in a ministry until we try it. We will never develop new abilities if we never try anything new. Not knowing anything about an area and not feeling qualified to do it are not excuses to not try it. It is always great if your gifts match up with an area of need within the church—serve your heart out in that area. If there is an area of need where no one is stepping up to serve, consider serving even it is not your gifting. Sometimes we need to consider the sacrificial service of Christ and be willing to stand in the gap. If our service never feels sacrificial, then I question if we are serving like Christ.

In ministry, we need to have hearts that are willing to serve the Lord without reservation. We should not only serve when it is comfortable, convenient, beneficial, and pleasurable. That attitude does not match the selfless service of Christ we should be living out. Let us serve because Christ humbly served others. Let us serve because Christ demonstrated His love for us on the cross. Let our service be a demonstration of our love for Him.

Consider carefully what you invest your time, energy, and money in. Beautiful houses, beautiful cars, beautiful gardens, and beautiful clothes will not last. The time will come when they will fall apart, fade, and amount to nothing.

On the day we stand before the Lord, we will not wish that we had spent more of our time, money, and energy on ourselves. "God is not unjust; he will not forget your work and the love you have shown him as you have helped his people and continue to help them" (Heb. 6:10). The Lord sees our service and He will not forget it. Life is short; let us live to serve Christ well.

JOURNAL QUESTIONS

1. In the past what reasons have motivated your service?

2. What holds you back from serving in different areas of your church?
3. How and why does the love of God and the gospel motivate your service?
4. How and why does the example of the way Jesus lived motivate your service?
5. When you look at your week and month, what are you investing your time, energy, and money in?
6. If strangers observed your life, what would they think are your priorities?

TEN

* * * * * *

HOW DO I HANDLE MY FEARS AND DESIRES?

> *I wish thy way.*
> *But when in me myself should rise,*
> *and long for something otherwise,*
> *Then Holy One, take sword and spear, and slay.*
>
> Amy Carmichael, *Rose from Brier*[1]

As women, we like five-year plans. We like five-year plans that actually turn out the way we plan. We love to be in control of our lives, to make a plan, and to execute the plan.

When it comes to relationships, sometimes the ten-year plan that we create in our heads does not translate into real life. If our ten-year plan includes a husband and a kid or two, it can be painful at the end of those ten years when there is no one. It can be even more discouraging when it does not look like it will happen any time soon.

For many, the older we become, the more we fear singleness might be a season that lasts the rest of our lives. The fear of being single for the rest of our lives is a very real fear, but we need to be wary of making decisions based on that fear.

Fear and desire can direct so many decisions. They are often intertwined together when we fear our desires will go unfulfilled. We desire to be married, and we fear it will never happen. Fear is a crazy thing. Well, fear will make you do crazy things or keep you from doing anything. People make a lot of bad decisions based on fear. We need to have faith that trumps our fear and submit our hearts and lives to the Lord and His will.

SUBMITTING DESIRES

Jesus submitted His life and will to the Father's in the garden declaring, "Your will be done" (Matt. 26:42 NASB). We need to accept whatever the Lord's will is for us, even if that does not include marriage. We do not mind submitting to His will as long as His will and our desires line up. Where the rubber meets the road, though, is where our desires and His will clash.

It would not be submitting if both parties had from the beginning been in agreement and had the same plan. Submission implies that there are two different plans, desires, wills, purposes, visions, or courses of action. It requires one person to submit theirs to another's.

We have a lot of desires. Some of our desires are for good things. Some of our desires are amoral (neither right nor wrong). Some of our desires are just plain sinful and self-ish. A desire for good things becomes sin if we develop a demanding spirit toward God to fulfill that desire. We can grow frustrated that God has not made our dreams a reality. This frustration is a good sign that we have more of a de-manding spirit than a submissive one.

At times, my spirit can get so out of whack. Internally, I feel like a two-year-old throwing a temper tantrum because I am so upset over not getting my way. I often turn the Amy Carmichael quote at the beginning of this chapter into my own personal prayer. I ask the Lord to slay anything in my heart that is not from Him. There is nothing wrong with my desire for marriage—unless I refuse to submit it to the Lord, and it becomes a demand.

In our prayers, we should examine the spirit in which we present our requests. Do you ask with a demanding spirit? Do you imply that the Lord is unjust or not good if He does not give you what you want? Do you ask with a "Thy will be done" mentality where you trust the Lord to do whatever is best? Do you hold onto your dreams, plans, and desires with a clenched fist or an open hand? Do you pray as a way to ask for His provision and to entrust your life to Him? Your prayers should flow out of a heart of faith because you trust Him.

Last year I realized I was praying because I did not trust the Lord. Sounds odd, I know. I was praying because I did not trust that God would do what was good if I did not pray. This had been going on for a while before I realized it. It was like I was trying to use prayer as a way to ensure I would get what I desired. I needed to resubmit and entrust my life to Him again.

I wish I could submit my dreams and desires to Him once and have it be permanent. My heart does not seem to work that way. Instead, I find it is an attitude I need to continue to reaffirm in my heart. Submitting my desires is sometimes not only day by day but also hour by hour. I do not want there to be any area of my life that I refuse to bring under His Lordship. If He is Lord of my life, then nothing is outside of His jurisdiction.

Beware of holding to a warped version of the gospel that does not preach crucifying any of your desires. "Those who belong to Christ Jesus have crucified the flesh with its passions and desires" (Gal. 5:24). It is not called crucifying because it is easy. It is called crucifying because it feels like death. Beware of your ability to justify pursuing your desires instead of crucifying them. Red flags should arise when we pursue our desires over the Lord Himself.

Oftentimes giving up all we have to follow Jesus is not on our radar, we just want Him to give us what we want. Only we tend to phrase it in a more acceptable way: God will give me *all* the desires of my heart. We want following Jesus to mean that we give up nothing, and He gives us everything we want. We do not think of the Lord as treasure in a field that we would sell all we have just to buy.

EVE'S DESIRES

As women, if we fear our desires will remain unfulfilled, it is tempting to take matters into our own hands. This temptation is what got women into trouble in the beginning. "When the woman saw that the fruit of the tree was good . . . pleasing . . . and also desirable, so she took . . . it" (Gen. 3:6). Eve had two options: (1) trust in the goodness of God to give her what she needed or (2) take whatever she wanted for herself. I have often felt like I was in Eve's shoes, seeing something good, desirable, and pleasing. My flesh says: "Take it." The world whispers: "Take it; if you do not, it may never be yours."

Like Eve, we can overlook the fact that ill-gotten gain takes away life; it does not give it (Prov. 1:19). Eve found out the hard way. When she pursued what her flesh wanted and took it for herself, it took away life.

It is not wrong to recognize that something or someone is

good, pleasing, and desirable. However, it is wrong to try to manipulate situations to obtain a romantic relationship instead of trusting God. We need to be convinced that He is a good Father who gives good gifts in His perfect timing. If we do not trust Him, there are always consequences. We will eat the fruit of our own ways and be filled with the fruit of our schemes (Prov. 1:31).

In the beginning Eve's life was as perfect as it gets. Yet she was still deceived into thinking that she needed something more. How much more is the potential for you to be deceived in this fallen world? What preceded Eve's sin was the belief that God was withholding something good from her, but was He? When you were younger was there ever something you wanted that you later realized was not as it appeared? What if what you think would be good now would really be bad—like turn to gravel in your mouth bad? Remember from Eve's perspective she thought the fruit was good.

The Israelites' Desires

The best thing for us is to keep the Lord Himself as our greatest desire. If we cultivate and feed a desire for other things, then we may find that the Lord is no longer our greatest desire. The Israelites' lives provide many examples for us to consider and take to heart:

> Now the people complained about their hardships . . .
> craved other food . . .
> the Israelites started wailing . . .
> "If only we had meat to eat . . .
> We were better off in Egypt" . . .

the Lord will give you meat . . .
until it comes out of your nostrils and you loathe it . . .
because you have rejected the Lord. (Num. 11:1, 4,
18, 20)

It is important to note that what the Israelites desired was not sinful. They just wanted meat to eat. Much of the time it is not our actual desires that are sinful. It is what we do with the desire and how we seek to gratify it, that can be sinful.

I want to be different than the Israelites, but I often do not feel different than them. They were complaining about their hardship. In my heart, I can complain about the hardship of being single when I want to be married. It is not meat that I crave, but a husband. Some versions say they were "wailing," others say, "weeping." There have been moments when my own unfulfilled desires have driven me to tears. The Israelites went as far as to say that they were better off in Egypt. In my darkest moments, I can think the same. It can be tempting to think I was better off before I started following Jesus, then I could pursue whomever. That thought almost makes me want to vomit because Jesus is always better.

Women whose desire for a husband is not yielded to the Lord are willing to compromise on the sort of man they date. If we think fulfillment is in the temporary, then our worldly desires will enslave us. In Numbers 11, the Lord gave them what they thought they had to have, and in the end they loathed it. The Israelites should have sought to be content, but instead they demanded something else. We should seek to be content with what the Lord has already given us.

I am absolutely convinced that Jesus is better, and I do not want to go back to Egypt. I also do not want a husband if it means that I will no longer be running after Jesus and pursuing His kingdom. Jesus has always been and will always be better than the best human husband. If I never marry, Jesus is enough.

In my mind, I know this is true. However, in the end, I can give way to fear, and I do not live out this truth the way I would like to.

One time I went to a prayer meeting at church, and subtly I was looking for a certain man. I caught myself and thought, "What am I doing? Whose face am I here to seek?" I realized I was looking for the wrong man's face. "My heart says of you, 'Seek his face!' Your face, Lord, I will seek" (Ps. 27:8). It is the Lord's face we should seek.

Throughout the Old Testament, God compares Israel to an adulterous spouse. Israel is always straying from her husband, the Lord. He tells the Israelites to "remember all the commands of the Lord, that you may obey them and not prostitute yourselves by chasing after the lusts of your own heart and eyes" (Num. 15:39). "Chasing after the lusts of their own hearts and eyes" would be a good way to describe the culture we have grown up in. Apart from Christ, we do not know anything else. When we become Christians, we are to stop chasing our lusts. As Paul told the Galatians, we are to crucify the flesh with its passions and desires.

The culture around us influences us more than we ever realize. One passage I have often thought about is the Lord's critique and judgment of the women of Israel in Isaiah.

> The Lord says,
> "The women of Zion are haughty,
> walking along with outstretched necks,

flirting with their eyes,
strutting along with swaying hips,
with ornaments jingling on their ankles.
Therefore the Lord will bring sores on the heads of
     the women of Zion;
The Lord will make their scalps bald."

In that day the Lord will snatch away their finery:
the bangles and headbands and crescent necklaces,
the earrings and bracelets and veils, the headdresses
and anklets and sashes, the perfume bottles and
charms, the signet rings and nose rings, the fine robes
and the capes and cloaks, the purses and mirrors, and
the linen garments and tiaras and shawls.

Instead of fragrance there will be a stench;
instead of a sash, a rope;
instead of well-dressed hair, baldness;
instead of fine clothing, sackcloth;
instead of beauty, branding.
Your men will fall by the sword,
your warriors in battle.
The gates of Zion will lament and mourn;
destitute, she will sit on the ground.

In that day seven women
will take hold of one man
and say, "We will eat our own food
and provide our own clothes;
only let us be called by your name.
Take away our disgrace!" (Isa. 3:16–4:1)

Isaiah rebukes and warns the women of Israel of what is coming. The young men will die in battle, so their ratio of men to women will be very skewed. Seven women will take hold of one man, all of them begging him to marry her. These women will be destitute and desperate for a husband. They will try to persuade the men by saying the men do not need to feed or clothe them. All they want is to be called by his name, so the disgrace and shame of singleness will be taken away.

There can be shame attached to singleness in that no one has found you worthy enough to choose you as their wife. The solution will never be to go find anyone who is willing to fill this void. The solution is to remember the gospel, who you are in Christ, and God's great love for you. If you remember this truth, you will never be desperate.

We all know women who clearly communicate who they like without ever actually saying it. Anyone paying attention knows exactly who she likes. The Lord faulted the women of Israel because they were "flirting with their eyes, strutting along with swaying hips" (Isa. 3:16). When it comes to trying to get a man's attention, women can be so manipulative. The more manipulative a single woman is—the less she trusts the Lord. Their finery was not the issue, their proud hearts were.

Often it is fear that prompts our actions. We are afraid if we do not play the world's game our desire for marriage will remain unfulfilled. But making decisions based on fear will never lead to faith-filled living. It is a dangerous place if we get to the point where we want our desires fulfilled, no matter the cost. The more discouraged we are, the more willing we are to compromise.

THY WILL BE DONE

Refusing to submit our desires to the Lord is not a good game plan.

> But my people would not listen to me; Israel would not submit to me. So I gave them over to their stubborn hearts to follow their own devices. If my people would only listen to me, if Israel would only follow my ways... you would be fed with the finest of wheat; with honey from the rock I would satisfy you. (Ps. 81:11–13, 16)

I find the phrase "gave them over" rather haunting. More than I fear not getting what I want, I fear the Lord giving me over to my desires. The Lord is not going to force you to submit your desires to Him. He is not going to force you to follow Him, or serve Him, or seek Him, or love Him, or listen to Him. He did not force the Israelites to do any of these things either. Israel *chose* not to do these things, often to the Lord's sorrow.

The Lord wants us to submit our hearts and desires to Him because He knows what is best. We often think we know what is best, and we are often wrong. This same phrase "gave them over" is also found in Acts 7:42 and Romans 1. As much as I want a husband, I do not want one if he only comes as a result of the Lord giving me over to follow my own desires.

Whatever other desires I may have, I must have a greater desire to yield my life to Lord. "There are only two kinds of people in the end: those who say to God, 'Thy will be done,' and those to whom God says, in the end, 'Thy will be done.'"[2]

One of the hardest things for me is this constant tension of wanting my dreams for a relationship to happen now. My desires, especially my desire for marriage, seem to be something I need to again and again submit to the Lord. On prayer walks, I have said many times, often with tears, "Lord, You have my heart. You have my life. Do what You will."

We can have great peace in submitting to someone we trust. The greater our lack of trust in the other party, the greater our apprehension. We are apprehensive because we are unsure if it will all turn out okay in the end. The more you trust the Lord, the easier it will be to lay your fears and desires before Him. Having a greater confidence that He sees you, cares for you, and loves you will enable you to trust Him. You can rely on Him regardless of whatever life brings or does not bring. He has shown Himself to be faithful and trustworthy, and you can entrust Him with your heart and life.

Do not give way to fear. (1 Pet. 3:6)

Journal Questions

(If you have avoided writing out the answers to the previous questions—make this one chapter where you force yourself to write them down.)

1. What are your greatest fears?
2. What are your greatest desires?
3. When was the last time you verbally submitted your life, heart, and desires to the Lord?
4. How do your fears or desires impact the choices you make and the way you live?

5. Do you struggle with trusting the Lord with your fears and desires? Why or why not?

ELEVEN

* * * * * *

How Can I Pursue Moral Excellence?

Whatever weakens your reason, impairs the tenderness of your conscience, obscures your sense of God, or takes off your relish of spiritual things; in short, whatever increases the strength and authority of your body over your mind, that thing is sin to you, however innocent it may be in itself.

Susanna Wesley[1]

Our culture's promotion of sexual promiscuity is out of control. The normalization of sexual sin in our culture has caused us to be quick to justify sexual sin in our own lives. We need to reevaluate our standards in this area, and we need to be careful not to set the bar too low.

Instead of striving to grow in moral excellence, we tend to settle for showing a little more restraint than the world around us. For many, it can be tempting to think that as long as I do not have sex, I have victory in this area. Certainly, that is a victory. However, I believe God's will for us is more than merely refraining from sexual activity outside of marriage.

In view of all this, make every effort to respond to God's promises. Supplement your faith with a generous provision of moral excellence, and moral excellence with knowledge, and knowledge with self-control, and self-control with patient endurance, and patient endurance with godliness, and godliness with brotherly affection, and brotherly affection with love for everyone. (2 Pet. 1:5–7 NLT)

In response to all that God has done for us, we are called to make every effort to pursue moral excellence in every area of our lives. Moral excellence is not limited to the subject of this chapter, but it certainly includes our sexuality.

Regardless of our sexual sin before we became Christians, we are all called to the same standards of moral excellence in Christ. The biblical call to a life free of sexual immorality and impurity does not only apply to those who came to Christ with their virginity still intact. Yes, victory over sexual sin is a tough battle, but this does not justify throwing in the towel and giving in to it.

This can be a tough area to navigate, especially if sexual sin was a part of your life before you became a Christian. In college ministry, I had many conversations on this topic with girls who were starting to follow Jesus. One girl, in reference to her virginity, used the phrase "that ship has long since sailed."

I know this is a hard topic, with deep wounds for many. This area is the source of many women's deepest regrets. Many women, with tears, have told me they wish they could take back so much of what they did when they were younger. If this is an area where you have regrets or continue to wrestle, I want to remind you that we have a great Redeemer.

He specializes in redeeming broken lives. If you are strug-gling, I want to encourage you to press on, fight the good fight, and continue to fix your eyes on Jesus. I hope we all continue to grow as we follow the Lord, but none of us will outgrow our need for a Savior.

Even though there were many women in Israel, Jesus spoke to an outcast Samaritan woman.[2] She had been married five times and was currently living with another man. Jesus told her that what she was really thirsty for was Him, and that He alone would quench her thirst (John 4). She had thought the next relationship would fill the void in her soul, but she was looking to the wrong source. Jesus is everything our souls are thirsty for.

Many of us live like this woman looking to the wrong source. Indulging in sexual sins is seeking to meet your emo-tional needs in a way that is completely disassociated from Christ. When all the while He is fully able to satisfy you if you would but look to Him. One of my favorite passages on this is in Psalm 63, "Because your love is better than life . . . I will be fully satisfied as with the richest of foods."

SEX AND THE BIBLE

When I first started reading the Bible, it amazed me that the Bible even talked about sexual sin. I had always assumed that the church made up the "do not have sex before you get married" rule much later. I could not imagine that the Holy Bible would actually refer to sex. As I started reading through the Bible, it was astounding how much God ad-dressed sexual immorality.

As it turns out, technically, God created sex. He does not consider it a taboo subject. Sex is meant to be a good thing that bonds a married couple together. Every kind of sexual activity outside of this context destroys the good gift that God intended sex to be within marriage.

In almost all of Paul's letters to the churches, he mentions sexual immorality. Many of them are very blunt in their wording. "Put to death, therefore, whatever belongs to your earthly nature: sexual immorality, impurity, lust, evil desires and greed, which is idolatry" (Col. 3:5). Apparently two thousand years ago, new believers came from a wide variety of sinful backgrounds too. Who would have thought? Clearly, sexual immorality was an issue in the early church. You do not tell someone to slay a dragon unless there are dragons. Paul addressed sexual immorality because it was an issue. The instructions in this verse are very simple, very clear: *put it to death*. There is not intended to be a "keep it as a secret pet" option. Often this is not a one-time, put-to-death choice, but instead a daily one.

There are gray areas about the specifics of God's will for our lives, but many aspects are very clear. It is never God's will for us to engage in sin. It is never God's will for us to engage in sexual immorality. Sex outside of marriage is never God's will for your life. Regardless of the fact that you think you are in a committed relationship, it is still not His will. "It is God's will that you should be sanctified: that you should avoid sexual immorality; that each of you should learn to control your own body in a way that is holy and honorable, not in passionate lust like the pagans, who do not know God" (1 Thess. 4:3–5). The Lord's heart for us is the same as well—that we would learn to control ourselves in a way that is holy and honorable. Things that are outside of this include but are not limited to: having sex before marriage (including having oral or anal sex), watching sex between others (pornography), having sex with yourself (masturbation), and fantasizing sexual encounters. There is no way to make a case that any of these fall within controlling yourself in a way that is holy and honorable.

"All who have this hope in Him purify themselves, just as He is pure" (1 John 3:3). I have moments where I wish certain verses were not in the Bible, so I could be ignorantly comfortable in sin. I think that for about two seconds, and then I recognize: no, Jesus is better. I do not want Him to leave me in my sin. Our target is to purify ourselves because He is pure. He does not only want us to refrain from sexual immorality, but also to pursue purity in every area of our lives. He wants us to live in a way that is honoring and pleasing to Him. We ought to seek to live a pure life because God has made us pure and holy in Christ.

We will never get married and regret an ounce of victory in this area that we have fought to achieve or maintain. Some of us may never marry. If we do not marry, when we die, we will never stand before the Lord and regret a lack of sexual sin in our lives either. While the world around you caves, do not follow suit.

BATTLE OF THE MIND

God's will for our sexuality encompasses our thoughts and hearts, not just our bodies. Often the greatest battles for victory are completely unseen by others—except the Lord, who sees it all. He knows our thoughts, and He sees every single moment of our day. Every single woman wrestles with her thought life. For many women, singleness is the area of her life that she would like to change completely. If this is her reality, at least she can dream up her perfect life in her head. Daydreaming and fantasies are often the areas where women struggle the most. For some, if this area goes unchecked, it can lead to other sexual sins.

Jesus said, "I tell you that anyone who looks at a woman lustfully has already committed adultery with her in his heart" (Matt. 5:28). When Jesus refers to lustful thoughts as adultery, He is expanding the definition of adultery and sexual sin to include sexual fantasies. He refers to lustful fantasies as sexual sin that we are committing in our hearts. All too often it is tempting to justify sexual fantasies because it is only in our head. But God judges the thoughts and attitudes of our hearts as well as our actions. We choose either to fight and turn our thoughts to something else or to feed our lusts.

For some women, the greater temptation is in daydreaming. Daydreaming, as well as sexual fantasy, is harmful to us, and not how God wants us to spend our time. Daydreaming of the ways the man you like might ask you out. Daydreaming of the conversations you would have with him. Daydreaming of dates you could go on, how he might hold your hand or put his arm around you. Daydreaming of where and how he might propose to you. Daydreaming of your wedding: the bridesmaid dresses, the flowers, your dress, your first dance song. Pretty soon you find yourself daydreaming of marrying a man who you are not even dating. One reason we do this is because it provides an escape from the painful reality that we are indeed still single.

One of my favorite depictions of this is in the movie *While You Were Sleeping*. Sandra Bullock sees a man every day at work and begins to tell herself that he is the man she is going to marry. He does not know her name. Most of the time, he does not even acknowledge her existence. She sees two men mug him and push him onto the train track. He is unconscious and she saves his life. At the hospital, he is in a coma but the doctor will not let her go see him because she is not family. She says under her breath, "I was going to marry him." A nurse overhears her and takes her to his room. His family comes in and the nurse tells the family that Sandra Bullock is their son's fiancée.

Out in the hallway, Sandra Bullock asks the nurse, "Why did you say that? I'm not engaged. I've never even spoken to the guy."

The nurse replies, "What? Well, downstairs, you said, you said you were gonna marry him."

Sandra Bullock explains, "Oh, geez, I was talking to myself."

The nurse responds, "Well, next time you talk to yourself tell yourself you're single and end the conversation."[3]

Sometimes we need to tell ourselves we are single and end the daydream for our own good.

We often want to justify these daydreams because they seem innocent. There is nothing sexually inappropriate with them. We are only imagining ourselves in a fictitious romantic relationship. In reality, even these daydreams are not as innocent and harmless as we try to make them out to be. Even daydreams are dangerous because they stir up in us a covetous heart and a spirit of discontentment. We all know one of the main commandments is to not covet (Ex. 20:17). How can you daydream of a boyfriend or husband and somehow still be obeying the command to not covet? In Philippians 4, Paul says that he has learned to be content even in want. If you constantly daydream about a life that is not yours, how can you expect to learn to be content?

The Bible sets forth rather strict verses to guide our thought life. There are two verses that bring deeper conviction in this area for me. "May the words of my mouth and the meditation of my heart be pleasing to you, O Lord, my rock and my redeemer" (Ps.19:14 NLT). We should strive to have what we are meditating on and thinking about be things that are pleasing to the Lord. "Finally brothers and sisters, whatever is true, whatever is noble, whatever is right, whatever is pure, whatever is lovely, whatever is admirable—if anything is excellent or praiseworthy—think about such things" (Phil. 4:8). I have always referred to this verse as the litmus test for my thought life. Whenever I try to justify thinking about something questionable, I look to this verse. For daydreaming or fantasies, you do not even get past the first test. Is it true? Tell yourself you are single and end it.

In whatever area of sin we wrestle with, we need to remind ourselves that: "Though the righteous fall seven times, they rise again" (Prov. 24:16). The worst thing we can ever do is to give up and stop getting back up. It takes time to break old thought patterns and build new ones. Do not give up pursuing a thought life that is honoring and pleasing to the Lord. You may try hard for a while and still fall into sin. The point is to be growing and making progress in this area. Sometimes that means baby steps, but at least you are still taking steps in the right direction. We need to rein in our thought life, not give our fantasies free reign.

The longer we remain single, we have to be wary of justifying sexual sin or a fantasy life. Indulging the flesh does not become biblically more acceptable over time. Paul said, "Make no provision for the flesh in regard to its lusts" (Rom. 13:14 NASB). Being unmarried longer than you want is never an excuse to indulge your flesh. Whether we remain single for five years or fifty, we must not make excuses to sin. Temporary gratification of sexual desires will never lead to lasting fulfillment. We must continue to pursue the holy and pure lifestyle to which God calls us.

WHAT ARE YOU STORING UP?

If you are serious about gaining victory in this area, you need to reevaluate what you feed your heart, soul, and mind. "An evil man brings evil things out of the evil stored up in him" (Matt. 12:35). Is what you are storing up hindering you from making progress in this area? If you eat several slices of cheesecake every night, you would not wonder why you struggle to lose weight. What you listen to, watch, and read will directly impact and influence your thought life.

Most of us grew up listening to secular music. Even those who grew up in the church rarely only listened to Christian music. Some of us need to reevaluate the messages that we are feeding ourselves through our music. Growing up on a farm, I naturally listened to country music. Rarely do I listen to it anymore, because a lot of country songs are about relationships. I am unable to listen to very many of them before I am daydreaming of being in a relationship.

The Internet has changed how we watch TV. Video streaming allows you to watch it whenever you want. These streaming websites are great enablers of our binge-watching habits. It is amazing the amount of time we can spend watching a TV series on Netflix. These days though, not many movies or TV shows keep the action out of the bedroom. Even family TV dramas often contain implied sexually immoral relationships. Sitcoms are often worse with the addition of crude humor and sexual innuendos. I am not saying you have to stop watching TV—however, some of us need to reevaluate what we are watching, or how much we are watching.

If your desire is to follow the Lord with a pure heart, then consider what you are consuming. Do not feed yourself what encourages a lustful imagination. If you have many nights in a week where you simply binge-watch the night away, it may be time to make a new plan. Perhaps swap out some nights with the ideas found in my chapters on feeding your soul and serving. You may need to consider canceling your subscription for a month or two, so you do not always feel that next episode calling your name. Too many of us waste too much time staring at a screen. For full disclosure, I do have Netflix and Amazon Prime, so I have those two sources of streaming always available to me, but I try to be careful with how I use them.

Not only do we need to use discretion with what we watch on the screen, but we also need to use discretion with what we read. Decades before bedroom scenes were normal on TV, they were common in romance novels. For me, before I became a Christian, romantic novels were my favorite books to read. The problem was many of them were not romantic novels as much as pornographic novels. If you depicted on-screen the details written, you would consider it pornography. I spent most of my free time in middle school reading these novels. In high school, I transitioned to the slightly tamer teenage and chick-flick novels. As I started regularly attending a church youth group, I switched over to Christian romance novels.

After I became a Christian, I started to see how my life did not line up with the life God called me to live. This led me to reconsider my fiction reading choices. With my active imagination, I knew it meant saying goodbye to novels containing sex scenes. I knew that there was no way to argue that they were beneficial to my life as I tried to follow Christ. Now, I am very choosy with the fiction that I read. It is helpful that I read far more non-fiction than fiction. For the fiction I do read, I do my homework to make sure it is not unwise for me to read it.

For many of us, part of the problem is we watch or read too much Jane Austen. Do not get me wrong—I love Jane Austen. I love the version of *Pride & Prejudice* with Colin Firth and can quote it probably more than the average girl. Simply because it is not vulgar, though, does not mean that it is good for your heart. The classic idyllic romantic stories can stir up discontentment and covetousness as much as the modern promiscuous licentious ones. If you are wrestling with contentment, watching a chick flick might not be a good idea, even if it is perfectly clean.

There are probably some reading this book who wish they could keep what they view restricted to even PG-13. The technology at our fingertips is a double-edge sword. In college, I lead a small group and discipled several younger women who were learning to follow Christ. More than one of these women came into college with a pornography addiction. One of the few things these women had in common was that in high school they had their own personal laptop. A majority of other girls did not get their own laptop until they came to college. One of the most dangerous and damaging things that technology has done is give unlimited access to pornography to teenagers. Of course, bad habits do not always start in adolescence and you can acquire them at any time.

The generation growing up with access to pornography in their pocket is going to have a lot harder time gaining victory in this area. At a very young age, they are beginning to use pornography, fantasy, and masturbation as a coping mechanism. Indulging in sexual fantasies can lead to a masturbation addiction with or without pornography.

Pornography is selfishly viewing another's body for your own sexual pleasure. This includes everything from sexually suggestive images of poorly clothed people to erotic videos. It comes in a wide range from soft to hardcore but none of it has any place in the life of Christian seeking to have a thought life that is honoring and pleasing to the Lord. The only person whose body God has blessed you to view and respond to sexually is your spouse. If you are single, there is no biblically acceptable substitute. Again, you need to learn to live a life of self-control that is holy and honorable.

Like pornography, masturbation is selfishly seeking sexual pleasure. It feeds your self-centered, selfish desires rather than crucifying them. It is self-indulgent and self-satisfying, rather than self-controlled and self-denying. "You are not your own; you were bought at a price. Therefore honor God with your bodies" (1 Cor. 6:19b-20). Masturbation is usually linked to fantasy and/or pornography. If you kick the pornography out of your life, if you learn to redirect your thoughts, if you no longer allow your mind to entertain sexual fantasy, then the temptation to masturbate will likely decrease over time. Even though the journey to freedom will be a long road with many ups and downs, it is worth pursuing. "Let us lay aside the deeds of darkness and put on the armor of light . . . put on the Lord Jesus Christ, and make no provision for the flesh in regard to its lusts" (Rom. 13:14 NASB).

Women wrestling with pornography tend to feel an extra dose of shame. In the church and culture, it is generally a stigma only associated with men. I still cringe when I hear a pastor imply that only men struggle with pornography. I know that it makes it harder for any woman in the audience who is secretly struggling with it to then confess it. Whatever we feel the most shame over, we tend to keep secret the longest.

If there is a woman reading this book that wrestles with pornography and/or masturbation but has not confessed it to anyone: my dear sister, you need to confess it. Sin flourishes if kept in secret. Do not struggle alone in darkness—bring it into the light. If we walk in the light, we experience purification from sin through Jesus (1 John 1:7). Keeping sin secret creates distance in all your relationships as you seek to hide your sin and yourself. It prevents you from being fully known and from feeling wholly loved. Find a woman in your church; maybe she is your small group leader, or maybe she is your pastor's wife. I know it will be hard to get the words out, but for your own sake, I urge you to confess it. You are not likely going to be able to break free on your own. You are going to need accountability. There are many good resources available,[4] but none will replace face-to-face small group accountability. Many who wrestle with pornography addictions have deep emotional wounds from their past that they need to address. Escaping the painful reality of life by turning to a fantasy world will never give you the outcome you truly desire.

What's Jesus's attitude toward pornography? Do you really want to know? In Matthew 5 when Jesus refers to looking at a woman lustfully as adultery, what was his suggestion for dealing with looking at a person and lusting after them? Gouge out your eyes (Matt. 5:29). That is actually what He told the people. Gouge out your eyes. Please, do not go running to find your scissors! But if Jesus suggests a radical solution, maybe you should consider something radical as well. If your smartphone is your greatest stumbling block, then consider downgrading to a dumb-phone. If your personal computer is your gateway, maybe you need to get rid of it, or only use it in public areas. You should have at least one filter on all of your devices. Have your accountability partner set the passwords. Another solution may be getting rid of the Internet at your house, or at least try unplugging the Wi-Fi for a week or a month. I know some may think they are unable to live without it, but the freedom will surprise you.

Back when I was in college, we would do something called a media fast. No secular music, no movies, no television, no Internet surfing, no social media for a weekend, a week, or a month. Sometimes we did them as a small group and sometimes people did it individually. Maybe these seem like radical suggestions, but at times drastic sin calls for drastic measures.

REDIRECT YOUR THOUGHTS

As I have been serving the Lord in singleness, I have realized that if I want to follow the Lord with a pure heart, then I need to filter what is coming into my heart. "A good man brings good things out of the good stored up in him" (Matt. 12:35). Once we have restricted the content of what we consume, it then becomes a mental battle.

Our focus needs to be on what we are turning our

thoughts toward. We will fail if the focus is on what not to think. We need to concentrate on the things we should be thinking about. The best defense is a good offense. What are you going to think about instead? What are you going to do in your free time? What are you going to do at the end of a stressful day? What are you going to do when you are bored? What is your game plan? I do not have magical answers for everyone. You need to think about your own game plan.

As for what you can turn your mind to, I do have one suggestion. Memorize some psalms. I have found it helpful to have something specific to turn to when I need to change the direction of my thoughts. Reciting psalms and thinking about the words have been helpful to me. I started doing this a few years ago when I went through some terrifying circumstances. During that time I read the Psalms in order to fall asleep. Eventually, I decided to memorize Psalm 27. I would recite it when I went to bed to battle fear and anxiety. When I would wake up from a nightmare, I would recite it until I fell back asleep. I also realized it was valuable whenever I needed to take any thoughts captive. Since then, I have also memorized Psalm 16 and Psalm 63. When my mind drifts to fantasyland, these are what I redirect my thoughts toward.

If we want to seek and serve the Lord with moral excellence, we need to reevaluate what we are feeding our hearts and minds in our free time. Think about whatever the temptation might be for you to indulge in whether it is pornography, romantic novels, TV, movies, or the Jane Austen classics. Do not feed yourself romantic stories in your free time and then wonder why you struggle with contentment in singleness. That is like shooting yourself in the foot and then wondering why you are not able to run very well.

I know there is a lot in this chapter that is easier to write than it is to live out. Making progress in these areas will not be easy. Even though each day the battle may be hard-fought, every little victory is worth it. God does not want you to be enslaved to sin. He is on your side to help and support you in this journey.

You must have a greater desire than the desire to experience the pleasures of sin. I desire to walk with the Lord for the rest of my life. I desire to live a life that is honoring and pleasing to the Lord. I desire to stand before the Lord and not have an overwhelming sense of dread and regret. I desire to look back and know that I fought the good fight, finished the race, and kept the faith. Sin will inhibit all of these. It makes me want to kick sin out my life. It makes me want to pursue a life of moral excellence.

JOURNAL QUESTIONS

1. How has sexual sin in the world around you encouraged you to set the bar too low in this area?

2. What are the negative effects (mentally, emotionally, relationally, and spiritually) of indulging in romantic daydreams, sexual fantasies, or other sexual sin?

3. What music, TV shows, movies, books, and online content are you consuming that feeds your struggle in these areas?

4. Would it help you to grow spiritually if you did some kind of media fast for a month? What good things could you store up and feed your soul during that time?

5. Have you ever memorized an entire psalm before? What psalm would you like to memorize? Why would memorizing it be beneficial to your life?

TWELVE

* * * * * *

WHO AM I WAITING FOR?

*Restlessness and impatience change nothing
except our peace and joy. Peace does not dwell
in outward things, but in the heart prepared to
wait trustfully and quietly on Him who has all
things safely in His hands.*

Elisabeth Elliot[1]

To me, the word "wait" has become a dirty four-letter word. I hate waiting for anything.

We want things now and we live in the time of instant gratification. Sometimes the longest we have to wait for something is the two days it takes Amazon Prime to deliver. If we have to wait weeks or months for something, it feels like a thousand years.

Some of us are waiting to see if this man will ask us to marry him. Some of us are waiting to see whether or not we will ever get married. And some of us have given up on the idea of getting married. All of us, hopefully, are looking ahead to the day we will see the Lord face to face.

Whatever we are waiting for, I want to encourage us to wait well, to wait patiently, and to wait on the Lord. Often when I am in a line, my focus is usually on myself. I get frustrated that I have to stand there for even a short amount of time. If my focus is not on myself, then I am usually only being critical of whomever or whatever is causing me to stand there. If I have to wait in a line to buy one item, I will contemplate putting it back and leaving. At the grocery store, I always think: "Why are there not more checkouts open?"

Last year on a trip to Oregon, I was standing in a long line at a donut shop. The line snaked around inside and had at least ten people lined up outside on the sidewalk. Multiple times I considered if donuts were worth this wait. Once I made it to the portion of the line inside the shop, I spent the whole time critiquing the employees in my head. Noting ten different ways the guys working could be doing their job twice as fast. The more critical I am, the less I am walking in the Spirit.

Last year, I reread *The Hiding Place* by Corrie ten Boom. Below is an excerpt from when Corrie and her sister, Betsie, were in line as they went through registration at a Nazi concentration camp.

> It was the end of the long day of standing, waiting, hoping. . . . And still we were not allowed to sit . . .

> "Betsie!" I wailed, "how long will it take?"

> "Perhaps a long, long time." Betsie replied. "Perhaps many years. But what better way could there be to spend our lives?"

> I turned to stare at her. "Whatever are you talking about?"

> "These young women," Betsie replied.

"That girl back at the bunkers. Corrie, if people can be taught to hate, they can be taught to love! We must find the way, you and I, no matter how long it takes . . ."

I slowly took in the fact that she was talking about our guards. I glanced at the matron seated at the desk ahead of us. I saw a gray uniform and a visored hat; Betsie saw a wounded human being.[2]

Betsie saw with spiritual eyes. She saw the opportunity the Lord had set before them to minister to the women around them. Instead of being critical of the guards, she saw them as people who needed to know the love of God. As we are waiting, we need to open our eyes and look around. There are other people surrounding us, and we have an opportunity to be a blessing right where we are.

We need to guard against developing a critical and bitter spirit. The best way to guard against it is to focus less on yourself and what you want. Instead, focus more on loving the people around you. The longer the wait, the more intentional we need to be about doing this. Do not just sit around wallowing, do something. Love others sincerely, and make disciples wherever you are.

Last year I felt the theme of my year became "waiting patiently," with an emphasis on patiently. I am horrible at waiting patiently. I even had a fortune cookie where the first two words were "Be patient." Many days, on the outside it might have looked like I was waiting patiently, but on the inside—it was a fierce battle. There were days filled with sorrow and tears of impatient frustration.

There is a section of verses in James 5 on patience, and it ends with a verse about Job. "You have heard of Job's perseverance and have seen what the Lord finally brought about" (James 5:11). We should consider Job and remember what God did in the end. After everything Job endured, "The Lord blessed the latter part of Job's life more than the former part" (Job 42:12). This should encourage us to be patient to see what the Lord will finally bring about in our lives.

WAIT ON THE LORD

Last year, I also realized my perception of who I was waiting on was wrong. When I find myself the most impatient, it is usually because I do not recognize I am waiting on the Lord. Instead, I only see I am waiting on a person. In the Psalms, David never said he was waiting for the enemy army to surrender, for Saul to die, or for the people to crown him king. Instead, David's attitude was to: "Wait for the Lord; be strong and take heart and wait for the Lord" (Ps. 27:14). In most verses, David emphasized waiting on *the Lord.*

When I remember my life is in His hands and I see I am waiting on Him, I tend to be more patient. The Lord's arm is not too short to act or move. "Since ancient times no one has heard, no ear has perceived, no eye has seen any God besides you, who acts on behalf of those who wait for him" (Isa. 64:4). If my life needed to be different right now, God could easily make it happen.

In singleness, we need to seek to wait on the Lord with our eyes on Him, trusting in Him. Our eyes should not be evaluating every single man for his spouse potential. We need to learn to be content to stay in this season of life as long as He has us here.

Our God will always be a God who acts on our behalf. Look at the cross: no greater act could be done for us. He may not always act according to our wants or wishes, but maybe our wants and wishes are not His will for our lives. They might be His will, but we need to wait for Him and His timing.

This life may not hold for us all we have dreamed. What is on the other side of it, though, will surely be worth even a lifetime of waiting. For on the day you stand before the Lord, you will not regret one second of patiently waiting on Him and trusting in Him. We may only be disappointed we did not trust Him more.

I have come to the conclusion that if the Lord tells me to wait, it is in my best interest to obey. While that is not shocking, I usually never default to thinking it is in my best interest. My default is to never wait if I have the choice. From my point of view, getting it now always looks to be in my best interest.

It would be horrible if the Lord never told us, "No," or 'Wait." It is not in our best interest for Him to give us whatever we ask for every time. We can only see our situation from one angle, but the Lord can see it from every angle. When He tells us to wait, we need to trust Him and be willing to do what He says.

There is a great picture of this in the Old Testament. A cloud guided the Israelites to either stay put or set out. "When the cloud remained over the tabernacle a long time, the Israelites obeyed the Lord's order and did not set out" (Num. 9:19). I am sure there were times when they were encamped at the same spot far longer than they wanted. They needed to stay until the Lord told them to move.

It is the same in our lives: sometimes the Lord has us encamped far longer than we would like to. We wish we could move on to the next phase in our lives, but that is not what He has for us right now. Wherever He wants me to be, that is where I want to be. I do not want to set out if He wants me to stay, and I do not want to stay if He wants me to set out. Sometimes to discern what He has for us, we need to wait on Him in prayer.

Spending time in prayer, seeking God's direction, and asking Him to show us what He wants us to do with our lives is always time well spent. "In the morning, Lord, you hear my voice; in the morning I lay my requests before you and wait expectantly" (Ps. 5:3). It is hard to keep praying when nothing changes, but we need to learn to persevere in prayer.

Often when we are the closest to giving up, deliverance is right around the corner. If only we would be willing to tarry and persist a bit longer. We wait on the Lord for the mountains to move, the waves to part, and our prayers to be answered. I want a greater willingness to wait on Him with patience and perseverance.

MEN WHO WAITED

I have come to realize I know nothing of waiting. The men in the Old Testament, their seasons of waiting lasted years, not months. What do I know of waiting on the Lord in terms of years?

Joseph was in prison for years and then there was a glimmer of hope that the cupbearer would speak on his behalf. "The chief cupbearer, however, did not remember Joseph; he forgot him" (Gen. 40:23). The cupbearer did speak on his behalf . . . two years later. It did happen, but clearly not in the time frame Joseph was hoping for. He sat in prison for two more years before he saw what he hoped for realized.

The additional time Joseph spent there before the cup-bearer spoke can be summed up in one sentence: "When two full years had passed" (Gen. 41:1). Actually, it is not even a full sentence. In the middle of waiting, though, two years feels like forever.

When we get to the end of our lives, we may have a different perspective. I wonder when we get to heaven, how many things will we casually look back on and say it took so many months or years for x, y, or z. At that time, it will not seem as if we waited that long at all.

In reference to Joseph's time in prison, it says, "Until the time came to fulfill his dreams, the Lord tested Joseph's character" (Ps. 105:19 NLT). There are seasons where we must endure hardship for an unknown amount of time. It is in those seasons that our character is tested. As patience wears thin, waiting brings out the worst in people. Will you keep doing what is right in your waiting or will you become discouraged and fall into sin?

Trials have a way of revealing and refining your character. You are not stretched or challenged when everything is easy. In instant gratification, your character is not refined. Trials are never pointless because in them is always the opportunity to grow in Christlikeness. In situations where I am required to wait, my need to grow in patience is exposed.

What do we know of waiting? In comparison to the saints of old, we know nothing. When time stretches on, we can consider their lives:

Abraham waited 25 years for Sarah to have a son.
(Gen. 12:2, 4; 21:5)
Isaac waited 20 years for Rebekah to have a son.
(Gen. 25:20; 25:26)
Jacob waited 7 years to marry Rachel.
(Gen. 29:20, 27–28)
Joseph waited in prison for many years.
(Gen. 37:2; Gen. 41:46)
Moses waited 40 years to see the Promised Land,
and then he didn't enter it, but only saw it
from afar. (Ex. 7:7; Deut. 34:1–7)
Joshua waited 40 years to lead the Israelites into
the land. (Ex. 24:12–13; Num. 13; Josh. 1)
David waited about 15 years to become king after
he was anointed. (1 Sam. 16; 2 Sam. 5:4)

The Lord made promises to these men, but then it took years to see the fulfillment of what He promised. The Lord revealed to Joseph in dreams that his family would bow to him, but he waited in prison for years before they came true. When Joseph was in prison, he had no idea how long he would have to remain there. We do not know how long our seasons of waiting will last. As we remain here, we must continue to trust the Lord.

David had to make the choice to trust the Lord again and again. The Lord could have killed Saul at any time in order to make David king. David knew that, and he did not kill Saul even when given the opportunity. He refused to take matters into his own hands because of his convictions. Instead, he waited on the Lord. Every single one of these examples waited years. Some of them waited decades.

When the Lord promised Abraham a son, I do not think Abraham had any idea how long it would be until he was born. The uncertainty of the length of the wait makes me feel more impatient. If I knew how long the wait would be, I feel I would be able to wait better. But if I knew how long the wait would be, I would not need to trust the Lord as much in the meantime. "And so after waiting patiently, Abraham received what was promised" (Heb. 6:15).

We tend to lose heart quickly when our waiting stretches past the first year. Waiting is hard when you think the end is right around the corner, but then around the corner, nothing changes. At every corner you get your hopes up, only to have them dashed. We sabotage our peace in the wait when we focus on what might come. Peace comes when we are waiting on Him, trusting in Him, and setting our hope on Him. God was faithful to them; He will be faithful to us. We should not measure His faithfulness to us by Him giving us what we want in our timing.

Some of us may not see the blessing we want in this life. Many faithful believers have gone before us who did not receive the blessings they wanted on earth.

> Some faced jeers and flogging, and even chains and imprisonment. They were put to death by stoning; they were sawed in two; they were killed by the sword. They went about in sheepskins and goatskins, destitute, persecuted and mistreated—the world was not worthy of them. They wandered in deserts and mountains, living in caves and in holes in the ground. *These were all*

> *commended for their faith, yet none of*
> *them received what had been promised,*
> since God had planned something better
> for us so that only together with us would
> they be made perfect. (Heb. 11:36–40)

God commended these people for their faith, but their lives were not filled with unicorns and rainbows. May we seek to have a faith like theirs, not living for this life, but for heaven. Our greatest longing should be for a closer relationship with God, not tangible blessings. Through all trials, let us trust God in the midst of all that is uncertain. God did not guarantee you a happily-ever-after marriage. As believers, He did guarantee us that we will go to heaven and that He will be with us forever.

JOURNAL QUESTIONS

1. Do you find waiting hard or easy? Why?
2. As you wait are you growing more critical and frustrated or gracious and patient?
3. How do trials and waiting grow your perseverance?
4. As you wait do you see the people around you as people to reach with the love of Christ?

THIRTEEN

* * * * * *

WILL IT ALWAYS BE SO HARD?

What if I never marry—will God then take
that desire away?
Perhaps He will. . . . Perhaps He will not, in
order that we may understand what it means to
be "poor in spirit"—aware of our essential
poverty and helplessness, having nothing to be
proud of, nothing that would encourage us to
think well of ourselves.

Elizabeth Elliot, *Quest for Love*

Even if you have a good grasp of everything previously written in this book, there will still be days where singleness feels hard. Days where it feels like death. Death of dreams. Death of desires. As a friend recently said, "Being single is not the end of the world. But you will feel like it is." There will be hard days, and that is okay. It does not mean that you are doing anything wrong.

Not every day is hard. There are some months where singleness is enjoyable. Months where having a husband seems overrated. I love the freedom of setting my own schedule, not having to shave my legs, only cooking when I feel like it, eating cereal for dinner and brownies for breakfast. Some days I easily count the blessings of singleness and relish the independence of it. Plenty of days, I can laugh lightheartedly at still being single.

Last year, I had coffee with two of my closest friends. Emily had been married for a little over a year, and Chrissy had just gotten engaged the week before. Naturally, we were celebrating with Chrissy and talking about her engagement story. The whole time Emily was not feeling well and eventually she confessed she was pregnant. It then became a double celebration. Chrissy was getting married, and Emily was pregnant. Of course, they asked what was going on in my life . . . *um* . . . *I'm going to paint my bedroom . . . a color called "Wheat Bread."* I actually did not realize the irony of the conversation until later that day. I died of laughter as I thought, "Some people get married, some have babies, and the rest of us are doing exciting things like watching paint dry." Actually, it was exciting to paint my bedroom the color of wheat bread because it had been lime green when I moved in. I love these women, and I was so excited for them. Sometimes you just have to laugh at your life. Embrace it and laugh.

I know some women struggle with others getting married and having children while they remain single. I do sometimes struggle when women who are several years younger than me get married. With friends who are my age or older, it is easy to genuinely celebrate their engagement, because praise the Lord, maybe there is still hope for me.

I have always wanted to have several little boys. Whenever one of my friends tells me they are pregnant, I always hope it will be a boy. If I ever marry, I would be perfectly content with only sons. Seeing a family with little boys is always a stark reminder of what is absent in my life.

GRIEVING DREAMS

Through the years, the fickleness of my own heart has been clear countless times. One day I can feel at peace and content in singleness. The next day I am in tears because this is gut-wrenchingly difficult. Sometimes I oscillate between peace and tears within an hour. At times, my peace and contentment with singleness can stretch into months, but eventually my emotions always swing back. I find myself back at square one, wrestling through all the questions in this book again. When that happens, I pause and remind myself of specific verses as I work through my feelings until I have a renewed grasp on truth. Our emotions can be messy as we walk through this trial. There is a grief and sorrow that accompanies singleness as we face the possibility that our dreams of a family may never happen. On many days my heart and soul feel heavy because my dreams seem more impossible as time passes. Some days I greatly desire the "normal life" of a husband and kids, and their absence is like an ache in my soul, a haunting feeling that something is missing.

Hard days end with moments where I lay in bed at night wondering if this is what the rest of life is going to be like. The roughest days are when I go to bed wishing I could wake up to a different life. Wishing the painful reality that is my life would somehow dissolve overnight. Would it not be lovely if trials could dissolve while I sleep? But I wake up and my life is the same with the road ahead unclear. I must trust the Lord with this new day and press on.

Last year, on a particularly rough day, this line popped into my head, "He considers their grief and takes it in hand." It kept rolling around in my head. At first, I was not sure if it was a verse from the Bible, a quote from a book, or a line from a sermon. I went home and look it up; it is Psalm 10:14. Most things we grieve are things we have lost. We also have to grieve things we thought were going to happen, but then they didn't. In singleness, this includes having to grieve the loss of the dreams we had planned for our lives. This verse is a comforting reminder to me that the Lord sees my grief, my pain, my sorrow, and the heaviness of my heart. He feels that heaviness like a weight He holds in His hand.

Whatever it is we are struggling with, it can be very tempting to try to give the impression that we are fine. In my mid-twenties, none of my friends seemed to want to acknowledge or talk about their emotions regarding being single. The closer that our age crept to thirty, the less re-strained we became in talking about the hardships in single-ness. Looking back, I wish we had talked more openly about singleness and our hearts sooner. It is hard to support one an-other when you do not talk about it.

When life is difficult, what we want most is empathy. In talking with other single women, I have found encourage-ment and solidarity. There can be thoughts, ideas, and emo-tions floating around in our heads that if we say them out loud to someone, we realize they are ridiculous. Sometimes, though, they are not ridiculous and are a mirror of what the other person is wrestling with as well. Walking through trials with friends only makes the friendships that much sweeter.

Before you conclude that you are totally fine with single-ness, ask yourself: Do you really not care? Or do you actually care quite a bit and have only hardened your heart? A lack of tears in my life usually points to a hardness of heart more often than anything else. It is easier to shut down my heart than to feel the pain.

TALK TO YOUR FRIENDS

One hard part of continuing to be single is that the older you get, the more of your close friends get married. In your group of friends, there may be a dwindling number who are still single. It can be hard to lament singleness to someone who is married because they seem to want to give you a one-line pep talk to cheer you up. Either: "Thirty is the new twenty!" or "Marriage is hard, so enjoy being single!" What you actually need, though, is for them to listen to you and to say "Yeah, that's hard." Do not give up talking to your close friends about wrestling with singleness. Hopefully seeing your continual heartache will prompt them to listen well and be sympathetic.

Again, these friendships are something we need to be intentional in cultivating. Barring unique circumstances, adults do not make new best friends in a month. Friendships also are not maintained over years, unless at least one of you is willing to constantly initiate. With your married friends, you will probably need to be even more proactive in initiating. It is not that your friend does not care, but her time is not her own anymore. There are many other demands on her time and many other people seeking her attention.

Some of our friendships may only be for a season. I love the idea of lifelong friendships, but it is not always possible. We may need to let go of some and build new ones. The point is we need to have a few close friends who know the nitty-gritty of our lives.

Whether your friends are single or married, it is important to be open and vulnerable about your struggles. Do not suffer in silence. Singleness can be hard. Life can be hard. The worst thing is to be in denial that it is hard and you are in pain. The second worst thing is to realize it is hard, be in pain, and suffer silently. If my friend is suffering and in pain, I long to come alongside her, walk with her, encourage her. It is hard to do that if I do not know what is going on in her heart.

Sitting with a group of about ten women last year, one woman pointed out that each of us had a desire for a good thing that was unfulfilled, whether a husband, a baby, a different job, etc. As I looked around the room and thought about each woman's life, I was amazed to realize it was true. We all had an unfulfilled desire for something good. It amazed me because we rarely talked about them. In order to support one another, we need to be more open with our emotions about the hard things in life.

Keeping things real with your close friends will help protect you from deceiving yourself. Sometimes what we need from our friends is a gentle rebuke or a not so gentle one. If we have become delusional and think that we are definitely going to marry a certain man, we might need someone to tell us that we are indeed still single and not in a relationship. Being open, honest, and real with our friends helps us to not lose sight of reality and our convictions. The more discouraged women become in singleness, the more likely they are to settle. The accountability offered through close friendships is a huge blessing.

Most of us start off with a long list of the attributes of our ideal spouse. Some lists do need to be pared down. As the window for having kids begins to close, we need to be careful that we do not pare it down too much. We certainly should not throw it out altogether. I understand the desire to get married and have kids creates a pressure to throw out convictions. Be careful. When we start to compromise, everything becomes a slippery slope. It can be tempting to go from a man who is wholeheartedly following Jesus to a man who at least says he a Christian. One more step to a man who is willing to go to church. Another step further to a man who is considering Christianity or seeking truth. Pretty soon you are willing to settle for any man who gives you a little attention. While we might need to compromise on his height or hobbies, we should not compromise on his heart to follow Jesus.

If you marry, God wants you to be equally yoked (2 Cor. 6:14). Who you marry will influence how you live. I would rather be single for the rest of my life, than marry someone who will pull me away from advancing God's kingdom. It will be difficult to run this race by myself, but at least I will still be running. Try running a three-legged race in the opposite direction as your partner and see how well you can run.

CONSIDER JESUS

Sometimes God asks us to do difficult things for the sake of His kingdom. One thing I have often thought of is the attitude of Jesus. "Jesus resolutely set out for Jerusalem" (Luke 9:51). "I must press on today and tomorrow and the next day" (Luke 13:33). Jesus knew He was going to suffer, be betrayed, and killed. He predicted it and told His disciples it was going to happen. Then, He willingly walked into it. I want to commit my heart, my life, and set my face like flint to follow Jesus no matter what. Even if my circumstances only go from bad to worse, I want to keep going. If marriage and children happen, or they never happen, I want to persevere in following the Lord.

Jesus was single. He did not cheat in His humanity. It is not somehow harder for me than it was for Him. He willingly gave up His life to the will of the Father. He told His disciples to "deny themselves" (Luke 9:23). This is the opposite of what is popular in our culture. Our culture encourages us to indulge ourselves, and we feel entitled to do so. Jesus did not walk around claiming what He was entitled to, and He was entitled to more than we can even fathom. If Jesus willingly gave up what He had the right to claim, then maybe we need to reconsider what we think we have the right to pursue. As Christians, we certainly are not entitled to indulge our flesh.

One reason some days are hard is because it feels like we are denying ourselves. We would rather try to twist freedom in Christ to mean we can do whatever we want, than embrace denying ourselves, taking up our cross, and actually following Jesus. Denying yourself was not something relegated to a select few, but was directed at whoever wanted to be Jesus's disciple.

I would like to note that denying yourself is different than claiming your emotions do not exist. Denying yourself implies that you recognize your desire for something else and you refuse to allow yourself to act on it. This is different than denying you have a desire for something else. It is not holier to deny having unfilled desires. Biblically denying yourself means refusing to satisfy all your desires, not refusing to recognize you have desires.

BEWARE OF BITTERNESS AND EXPECTATIONS

The longer you have unfulfilled desires, the harder some days will feel. It is important that we do not allow hard days to translate into a hardness of heart. None of us are immune from our hearts growing hard and bitter toward the Lord. You can choose to follow the Lord, do what is right, serve your guts out, lay your life down, build His kingdom, but nothing might turn out the way you dreamed, planned, hoped and prayed. In singleness and other trials, there is the potential to get bitter at God.

Recently, my youngest sister, who is a little over ten years younger than me, asked me, "How do you feel about being single? Because if I were you, I think I would be bitter at God, because you've done what is right for so long and you are still single."

I half-smiled at her depth of insight and replied, "Yeah, I've been there. But ultimately Jesus is better, heaven is coming, and I want to live for Him."

Often the underlying cause for bitterness is that we feel the Lord has, in some way, wronged us. Unintentionally, I can fall into thinking I will follow the Lord, do what is right, and He will bless my life the way I want. I tend to think that Him blessing my life will look like Him fulfilling my dreams and desires. This may seem silly on paper. Often our emotions do seem silly when written in black and white. If you think back to a time when you have been angry or bitter toward the Lord, the root of it was likely in something not turning out the way you thought it should. On hard days, there is a potential for me to sling pointed accusations at the Lord.

We are not the only ones who question the Lord when there are hardships in our lives. John the Baptist sent his disciples to ask Jesus, "Are you the one who is to come, or should we expect someone else?" (Luke 7:19). John the Baptist had done everything right. He advanced the kingdom of God and prepared the way for the Messiah. He preached repentance and baptized countless people. When he stood up to Herod and spoke truth, Herod had John the Baptist arrested and thrown into prison (Luke 3:19–20). After a while, John the Baptist began to question whether Jesus was indeed the Messiah. Certainly the Messiah would not leave him in prison. John the Baptist was not the first person, nor the last, to question God based on what He allowed to happen. The Lord's response to John the Baptist will be the same as His response to us. "Blessed is anyone who does not stumble on account of me" (Luke 7:23). There is a potential for any of us to stumble in our faith based on what the Lord does not do for us.

We need to be careful of having unrealistic expectations in following the Lord. It is craziness for us to expect only what is good. It is craziness for us to expect that everyone's dreams and desires will all be fulfilled in this life. Especially when the New Testament constantly references troubles, hardships, persecutions, difficulties, and trials. John the Baptist was eventually beheaded (Mark 6:21–29), and Jesus did nothing to try to intervene or stop it. In Acts, both Stephen and James were killed (Acts 7:59–60; 12:2). I am betting that was not exactly what they envisioned for their lives.

The life of Jeremiah is also a great example of how things do not always work out the way we want. Jeremiah was beaten, put in stocks, imprisoned in a dungeon, thrown into a cistern, and imprisoned in the courtyard of the guard (Jer. 20:2; 37:16, 21; 38:6). We need to be careful of picking verses that promise what we want and building a theology that is irreconcilable with the lives of Jeremiah, John the Baptist, Stephen, and James. The promises of the Bible apply no more or less to these men's lives than they do to your life. Their lives were not smooth and easy; you should not expect yours to be either.

Although, I am sure that once these men were in heaven none of them thought that the Lord had treated them unfairly. No matter how hard our lives are here, I do not think we will either.

Regardless of what happens, we can rest assured that He is not malicious in what He allows in our lives. He sees better than we do. He knows better than we do. His goodness governs all that He does and does not do.

It is hard when I follow the Lord and my desires remain unfulfilled. In immense heartache, I have held onto this verse: "He restores my soul" (Ps. 23:3 NASB). The fulfillment of my dreams will not restore, nor satisfy, my soul. The Lord alone can do this. Do not deceive yourself into believing that the fulfillment of your desire for a husband will resolve everything. Remember, our hope should be in the Lord Himself and in heaven. Our longing to see our dreams fulfilled should never trump our longing for more of Jesus.

Whatever happens on the road ahead, I know His grace is sufficient. If I am single for six more months, six more years, or the rest of my life—His grace is sufficient. He is able to give me strength and to carry me through whatever this life holds.

Regarding anger and bitterness toward the Lord, the best thing you can do is to remember the gospel. You have been given and granted so much in Christ. Hopefully, you have a deeper understanding that God sees you, cares for you, and loves you. As I said earlier, when you find yourself wrestling with these questions again, work through them and renew your understanding of what is true. Sometimes we need to pray many times on hard days in order to process through them in a healthy way. I hope you will use the thoughts in this book to fight against bitterness in your heart on hard days.

JOURNAL QUESTIONS

1. Why does singleness feel hard for you?
2. Do you allow yourself to grieve the loss of your plans or dreams not coming true?
3. Do you have a few close friends who know the nitty-gritty of your life?
   a. If not, how and with whom can you develop that type of friendship?
   b. If yes, how can you be intentional about keeping things real and sharing your heart?
4. "Whoever wants to be my disciple must deny themselves and take up their cross daily and follow me" (Luke 9:23).
   a. In what ways do you deny yourself in order to follow Jesus?
   b. Have you made a decision to follow Jesus no matter what happens?
5. How often do you oscillate between good days and hard days? What are your go to Bible verses on hard days?

FOURTEEN

* * * * * *

HOW DO I HANDLE FAMILY AND HOLIDAYS?

*It must be a great consolation to you
to have a home . . . however remote,
or however seldom visited, still it is
something to look to.*

Anne Brontë, *Anges Grey*

Family. There are a lot of emotions tied up with that word. They love you. They mean well. They have good intentions. Bless their hearts; at least sometimes they are good for a laugh.

No one has a perfect family. Most families are bittersweet—sweet moments mixed with bitter ones. On the whole, I have been extremely blessed when it comes to family. The sweet has always outweighed the bitter. The older I become the more I appreciate my family.

Certain relationships can be difficult, but family is for life. My siblings will be my siblings for the rest of my life. I want to be quick to forgive, and I want to invest in those relationships. I do not want us only to be family, but also I want us to be friends. It does take two people to make a friendship. This might not work out for everyone, but it is important to try. "If it is possible, as far as it depends on you, live at peace with everyone" (Rom. 12:18).

Family members can be both your best friends and your worst enemies. Sometimes the difference is determined by the choices we make in our attitude and responses. "The wise woman builds her house, but with her own hands the foolish one tears hers down" (Prov. 14:1). Choose your words and attitudes wisely.

Conversations with family regarding our singleness are always interesting. In the next six months, if someone questions my relationship status, it will be my family. The first years of answering the questions about if there was a special guy in my life were painless. After years of the same answer, though, it is not as easily swallowed.

In all honesty, the single people I know dread their family's continuous questions of their relationship status. Thankfully social media has helped to decrease some of this. It allows my extended family to check my relationship status at any time.

For some people, it is a default question to ask when you have not seen someone in a while. If possible, I try to graciously end my response by saying, "If there ever is a significant other, I will be sure to let you know." Hoping to encourage them not to ask the next time I see them.

One reason why questions from family and friends are painful is because it feels like they are implying that it is not okay for you to be single. The older I get, the more I feel this imaginary weight of implications that I really ought to be married by now. They usually are not trying to imply something is wrong with me or that I am doing something wrong. It just feels like it.

Some people are actually trying to imply that about our lives. Some of us may even have family who are straight up saying those things, and who will even offer their advice to try to help you. However, most people ask because they genuinely care about what is going on in your life. They would like to check if you have a significant other that you are hiding somewhere.

In recent years, I have started to sense my family forming the assumption that I do not want to get married. They have started wording things as if they are trying to convince me that marriage is a good idea. Trust me, I think marriage is a great idea, and I would love to get married someday.

Regardless of what they are straight up saying or simply implying, it is important for us to be confident in our identity in Christ. Family members questioning our relationship status can bring out our insecurities. We battle these insecurities by remembering the truth of who we are in Christ. He greatly desires a deep and intimate relationship with each one of us.

It is easy to let people's comments roll off your back if you are confident the Lord sees you, cares for you, and loves you. If you question these things, then your doubts will be fed by conversations with your family.

Family can be this constant source of pressure to hurry up and get married. It surprises me that for some singles, their family is very vocal about urging them to compromise. Their parents are the ones desperate for them to get married. Their extended family is trying to offer creative suggestions and helpful ideas. Their family has set up marriage as the end all be all. If this is you, smiling and nodding may not cut it. You will need to give a deeper explanation about your convictions. The greater the pressure you face, the more you need to encourage yourself and remind yourself of what is true.

Over the years as other family members have stopped

asking me about my relationship status, I can always count on my grandmother to ask. I have heard the story of her and my grandfather many times. She was twenty-one when they married, and in her day they considered that on the verge of being an old maid.

My grandmother can best be described as one of my best friends in an old person's body. Seriously, she has been my longest confidante. She only had sons and I am the oldest granddaughter. I spent a lot of time at her house when I was growing up. In high school when I went over there, we would sit at her kitchen table drinking tea (with lots of sugar). I would pour out all my teenage angst to her and she would patiently listen.

I wish I had written down our conversations over the past decade about my lack of a boyfriend. It would have been great material for this book. In many of our conversations, it is hard to contain my laughter.

Last year she asked me, "Is there no one that turns you on?" Even I can't maintain a straight face when my eighty-year-old grandmother asks me that. She has asked me different versions of that question many times.

Sometimes our conversations are more serious. My grandmother, while she questions me the most, has been the one to show the most genuine concern. One time I remember her telling me, "I don't want you to be alone forever." *Me neither Grandma, me neither.*

When I was in my late twenties, my grandmother faithfully prayed for a husband for me for two years. Then she told me she had determined God said no. I have often looked back on this conversation and thought: "Maybe my grandmother was right." Although, her perceived answer from God has not deterred her from continuing to ask me if I know any good-looking boys.

HAPPY HOLIDAYS

Holidays are just rough no matter which way you slice the cake. We all secretly wish someone would desire to serenade us with a rendition of "All I Want for Christmas Is You." Every time we go home for a holiday, we have an in-your-face reminder of our singleness because we have no significant other to bring with us. We often tell ourselves that maybe by this time next year we will have someone to bring.

For some people, the holidays bring an even more heightened reminder, as their family celebrates a combined Thanksgiving and Christmas in early December, and then on Christmas Day, they have no one to spend it with.

If you find yourself alone on holidays, try to find others who are in a similar situation and plan something with them. There may also be another family who would gladly welcome one more to their festivities. You could also look for non-profits in your area that are in need of volunteers on holidays and help out there.

When I am going to see my family for the holidays, the most important thing is for my heart to be in a place where I am okay with being single. If I go into these days discontent and frustrated, my family's questions and comments will only compound my emotions. It is important to prepare your heart for holidays with family by spending extra time with God. Be intentional about feeding and encouraging your soul. If you are discontent and frustrated with singleness, the Christmas romantic comedies on Netflix will not be helpful.

Holidays can make the questions feel heavier because

you have to answer the same questions, multiple times in one day. The larger the family, the more times you have to answer questions about your relationship status. It is especially difficult if you have to answer six different versions of the same question in four hours. Maybe I should get a nametag with "Still rockin' out the single life" written on it. Just kidding, I know they ask because they want to know about my life.

As painful as the holidays can be for a single person, I love the holidays, because I really love my family. My parents are still married, and both sets of my grandparents are still married. They all live within fifteen miles of one another. It has always made holidays relatively simple for me. I go home for every holiday weekend and see my whole extended family. A year or two ago, my mom asked me, "Are you coming home for Thanksgiving?"

I do not know if she expected me to say, "Actually, I have a boyfriend in the closet and I'm going to spend Thanksgiving with him and his family." I just gave her a puzzled look and laughingly asked, "Where else do you think I'm going to go?"

She said, "I'm sorry, that's not what I meant," and gave me a hug. I think she thought maybe I would do something with my friends.

SINGLE AT A WEDDING

If holiday gatherings are interesting, family weddings are the spice of life. Weddings, in general, can be hard if you are single and long to be married. If it is a friend's wedding, I normally have other single friends to go with. There is no such luxury at family weddings.

Since I have three younger siblings, I usually hang out with them at family weddings. At my cousin's wedding reception a few summers ago, things were different. I was the seventh wheel. Is that a thing? One of my sisters is married and my other two siblings brought dates to the reception. There is nothing like being the oldest and the only one without a date. It was really fine until things took a turn for the worse. I remember the moment very clearly.

My stomach filling with dread as the DJ announces, "Will all the single ladies please make their way to the dance floor for the bouquet toss?" People start looking around the room. My dread deepens as no one moves.

At first, I think: How did I not see this coming, and why am I not hiding in the bathroom right now?

Secondly, I think: Is it too late to go hide in the bathroom now?

Unfortunately, I am at the table closest to the DJ and about the furthest from the bathroom. In fact, I would have to cross the dance floor to escape to the bathroom.

Maybe if I just sit here quietly, I can get out of this.

Again the DJ announces, "Come on, are there no single ladies?" The dance floor is still empty, except for the bride.

My family starts pointing me out. I kid you not. My father and brother start making large gestures pointing at me.

Traitors.

Can a hole open in the ground and swallow me up? An ever-increasing number of my extended family members start pointing at me and calling me out. *I love you all too.*

It is clear there is no option to hide or even remain seated. The DJ understands what they are saying and calls me out on the microphone. Yep.

I reluctantly walk to the dance floor to join the half a dozen girls that are all under thirteen. They clearly all think a single ladies bouquet toss is the highlight of the reception.

Thankfully two of my cousins, who are nineteen and twenty-three, join me. They are as enthusiastic as me to be out here. Bless them. Not sure if they took pity on me or were also forced, but bless them. We stand practically motionless during the bouquet toss and let the little girls fight over it.

If being the seventh wheel was not enough to accent my singleness, this highlighted it for the whole room. My own eighteen-year-old sister did not even join me on the dance floor, but hid behind the excuse of holding someone else's baby. *How about next time you run and hand me the kid?* I will take any excuse.

Honestly, it was fine; the humiliation lasted only a few minutes. A few days later, I laughed about it with my other single friends. However, next time I really do need to plan ahead and hide in the bathroom.

I wish I had some perfect response to pass on to you for how to answer your family's questions, but I do not. At times, the best you can manage to do is smile and nod, or shake your head and say nope. When possible, I try to use it as an opportunity to point to the Lord. One way is to say: "It's giving me a chance to pursue knowing Jesus more." It can also be an opportunity for me to explain my convictions to marry a Christian who is wholeheartedly following the Lord. Not every conversation provides this opportunity, but when it does I try to weave it into my response.

Family time and holidays can be hard, especially if we are trying to ignore the reality that we are single. Oftentimes, we try to distract ourselves from facing this reality. Then, when family directly asks us about it, it is hard to answer their questions. Do not avoid addressing the pain and heartache of being single. You are not doing yourself any favors.

It is important to be at a place where you are at least okay with being single when you head to a family holiday or wedding. Take time before you go to work through your emotions with the Lord. Seek to be at a place of peace with singleness. Happiness and contentment are no more found in marriage than they are in singleness.

JOURNAL QUESTIONS

1. What has been your family's response to your singleness?
2. In the past, how have your family's questions and comments impacted your feelings about singleness?
3. What is your game plan for handling questions from your extended family?
4. Reflect on the last holiday season, family wedding, or weekend home: Was your heart in a good place going into it? Did little comments and questions stick with you or were you able to let them go?
5. What are you thankful for about your family? How have they been a blessing to you?

FIFTEEN

* * * * * *

WHO ARE MY ROLE MODELS?

*I wish . . . that even a tenth of the trouble
we take to fit our circumstances to our
desires were used in fitting our desires to
our circumstances.*

Charles Spurgeon

In Genesis 2, it says that God created woman to be a suitable helper for man. The only problem is no one seems to want my help. *Well . . .* I thought that was funny; maybe you would think it was funny too if it was not so painfully true.

The main dreams for our lives may revolve around getting married, buying a house, and having kids. When we think those things will happen, we look to examples of people who are doing that well. We set up women who balance following the Lord, loving their husbands, and juggling many kids as role models. Married women are great roles models, but if our lives look nothing alike, they are not the best ones for us.

There is nothing wrong with wanting to get married, buy a house, and have kids—but making that your only dream is not a good idea. Especially if you are still single five, ten, fifteen, or twenty years from now. At some point, you will realize that you idolized being a wife and mother too much, and you will need to find some new role models and new dreams.

The great news is that there is an endless list of both of these that have nothing to do with being a wife or a mother. As I have wrestled with singleness, one of my greatest sources of encouragement has been the writings of other single women. This has come from books or blogs written by single women as well as biographies written about single missionaries.

Throughout the centuries there have been many amazing single women who are heroes in the faith. In one sense, I desire to build a list of single women who have faithfully followed the Lord, whose example I can look to for encouragement. I am going to mention a few and give a brief outline of their lives. This is by no means a complete list, but I want to help get you started.

MY FAVORITE FIVE

Over Christmas break in college, I read *The Hiding Place* by Corrie ten Boom for the first time. It is her autobiography centered on when her family hid Jews in their home in Nazi-occupied Holland. Even though the book is an autobiography, it reads more like a fiction book. Corrie and her sister, Betsie, never married and lived at home with their father until the Nazis arrested them. The book includes a chapter about Corrie's relationship with the man she hoped to marry.[1] I have read *The Hiding Place* four or five times, and every time, I have been greatly encouraged by Corrie's life. There is also a sequel to it called *Tramp for The Lord*, which is about her international ministry after the war.[2] Let me just say: it will erase any excuse anyone has of being too old to start doing something for the Lord.

One of my favorite authors is Elisabeth Elliot. She was a prolific writer and speaker. She was married three times, so she does not exactly qualify as a single woman, although her first husband, Jim Elliot, was martyred in Ecuador twenty-seven months after they were married. By the time Elisabeth turned thirty she was a widow.[3] As a young widow, she took her daughter and moved in with the tribe who killed her husband.[4] She did not marry her second husband until she was in her early forties, and he died less than five years later from cancer. In total, by the age of fifty, she had been married for less than seven years.[5] She wrote the classic *Passion and Purity*, which is on dating and her relationship with Jim, as well as its sequel *Quest for Love*, which answers questions from her readers.

A woman that Elisabeth Elliot greatly admired was Amy Carmichael. Elisabeth wrote a biography about Amy called, *A Chance to Die*. Amy moved to India before she was thirty years old and spent the rest of her life there. Originally, she spent her time as an itinerant evangelist. When she saw children being dedicated to temples and raised to be prostitutes, she started a ministry to rescue these children. Eventually, she built an orphanage, the Dohnavur Fellowship, which is still in operation today.[6] Amy also wrote many books about the Christian life and her missionary work.

I also learned about Rachel Saint through the writing of Elisabeth Elliot. The Auca Indians killed Rachel's brother, Nate Saint, along with Elisabeth's husband, Jim. Before her brother's death, Rachel was also in Ecuador learning the language from a woman who had left the tribe. Two years after the men's deaths, Rachel went with Elisabeth to live with the tribe.[7] Many in the tribe became Christians, including the men involved in killing the five missionaries. Rachel Saint stayed with the tribe for the majority of her life and eventually translated the entire New Testament into their language.[8]

We must choose what we will spend our lives accomplishing. Lilias Trotter had the potential to be a great and influential artist. Her mentor told her that in order for that to happen, she would need to give herself completely to her art. Knowing that she could not devote herself to both her art and ministry, she decided to give herself first and foremost to ministry. Later at age 35, Lilias moved to Algiers to be involved with the missionary work there. Until the time of her death, she established and managed mission stations throughout Algeria.[9]

My intent in noting these women is not to imply all single women should become foreign missionaries. Before her arrest, Corrie worked as clocksmith in her family's watch shop. In fact, she was the first female watchmaker licensed in Holland. She held weekly Bible studies in her home for the mentally handicapped. Her father, sister, and herself took in a number of orphan children and raised them.[10] Elisabeth came back from the jungle and spent most of her life writing and teaching. Long before Amy went to India, she was sharing Christ with women, who were working in the mills and factories. She taught weekly Bible study lessons to a large group of young women.[11] Rachel worked with alcoholics for twelve years at a mission in New Jersey.[12] Lilias volunteered to work with young women through the YWCA in London. This included working with prostitutes to teach them a vocational trade and about the gospel.[13] If the previous paragraphs make you feel like you need to go somewhere else, please know that was not my intent. You do not need to go anywhere to find people to love and serve. There are people you see every week who need to hear the gospel just as much as people on the other side of the world.

This is a short and incomplete list of single women to whom we can look to as role models. They are women whose lives I have found encouraging and challenging. Throughout the centuries and especially in the past fifty years, single women have lived amazing lives for the Lord. In this day and age, we also have the added benefit of accessing a wide variety of blogs. The majority of Christian bloggers are wives and mothers, but there are also a growing number of single women writing blogs. These blogs have been immensely encouraging to me. I want to refrain from listing specific blogs, given the rapidly changing nature of their lives and the Internet. We also need to exercise discernment with what we read. Just because something is in a book, article, or blog does not make it true. A lot of Christians have unbiblical opinions. The Bible should always be our main source of encouragement and the truth through which we filter everything else we read. However, reading about other single women has also spurred me on in my walk with the Lord.

New Goals, New Dreams

The point is to not set up moms and wives as our only role models but to find some single women who have been faithful in following the Lord. If they can make it decade after decade honoring and serving the Lord, then I feel encouraged that I can do the same. Being a wife and mom is great, but that should not be our only goal in life. I just want to encourage us to have some holy ambition for our lives. It is too small a thing for our only ambition to be to watch another TV series on Netflix. Outside our door is a hurting and broken world that desperately needs to know the love of Christ. Sometimes I wonder if the Lord ever thinks: "All of these women just want to be wives and mothers, but I am looking for some women to be warriors in other arenas as well."

Allow yourself to dream a little or a lot. If you do not get married, what might God want you to do with the next ten, twenty, thirty, or forty years of your life? For some of you, the answer to this question might be crystal clear. I will assume that a few people will be in my boat. I can think of three or four big things I would love to do, but they are mutually exclusive. Sadly, I will only be in my thirties once, and there are a limited number of things that I can do in this decade of my life. We need to make decisions, but let us make them in prayer, filtered through His Word while seeking wise counsel.

There is a world of opportunities for you out there. Some of you might want to pursue going into full-time foreign missions. Others might want to be well grounded here and become involved with reaching the next generation. Perhaps you should get your master's degree or a doctorate. If the thought of continuing down your current career path for the next twenty years makes you nauseous, then maybe you need a new one. There are also a wide variety of ministries within your church to get involved in. If you have a heart for a ministry that is not currently offered, you could start something. In the community, there are mentoring programs, food pantries, homeless shelters, animal shelters, and other volunteer opportunities you could pursue. Do not spend the next decade thinking about how you have always wanted to get involved in this one thing. If you want to do something, actively seek out taking the next step. Consider taking some friends along with you, that way if things do not go well, at least you will have good company to laugh with afterward.

Sometimes I wonder what the missionaries in heaven think of how we spend our time with all the modern conveniences available to us. When I read *These Strange Ashes* by Elisabeth Elliot, it surprised me how much time the missionaries spent baking bread and washing clothes by hand.[14] There was no other way. They had to spend so much of their day just taking care of the basic necessities. In previous centuries, missionaries would have loved to have our modern conveniences in order to spend more time on the gospel. Today, people on opposite sides of the world can easily communicate with one another, and flying there is simple. These are luxuries that, two hundred years ago, missionaries could not fathom. They instead spent months on ships to get to foreign countries and waited months to receive letters.

It would surprise previous generations of believers how we spend our lives or more accurately, how we *waste* our lives. "Where there is no vision, the people are unrestrained" (Prov. 29:18 NASB). If you have no dreams of what you want to do with your life, then you will put forth no effort to get there. In order for us to not waste our lives, we have to have some purpose that we are actively pursuing.

If the women mentioned earlier had been married with kids, then their lives would have looked vastly different. There is an opportunity cost that works in both directions. We have opportunities to do things as singles that we would otherwise not have the availability to do. If I remain single, it will probably be because the Lord has other things for me to do in advancing His kingdom. Things I could not or would not do if I were married with kids.

As I look back on the past several years of my life, there are countless things that I would not have done if life had gone the way I wanted. Every year I have gone on short-term mission trips to a foreign country and have chaperoned several teen retreats and trips. Those are big things, but there are many smaller things in my day-to-day life that also would not happen if my circumstances had been different. Dinners with women, conversations with roommates, trips with friends, and discipleship of younger women—all these would have been impacted. There may be things we have been set apart as singles to serve the Lord in that we would not do if we were married.

I do not want us to make the mistake of pursuing life, satisfaction, and joy in some experience or accomplishment in this world. It can be deceiving to think that finding our unique purpose will fulfill us. Life, satisfaction, and joy are found in Jesus. If you look for them in experiences or accomplishments, you will always go from one thing to the next for what they offer is fleeting at best. There is a big difference between doing things to seek self-fulfillment and doing things because you are fulfilled in Christ. The women mentioned earlier believed life, satisfaction, and joy were found in Jesus. Because of Him, they dared to take risks and accomplished great things. They were not looking for life, satisfaction, or joy; they had already found it.

We are truly surrounded by a great cloud of single women who have lived amazing lives serving the Lord and loving people. As single women, let us look to these women for encouragement as we seek to press on, to fight the good fight, and to finish the race strong. Read their books, read their blogs, and dream of how you could spend your life advancing God's kingdom. God has good things for His people to accomplish, so let us not waste our lives wishing we were married. Let us live fully for God.

JOURNAL QUESTIONS

1. How have you set up marriage and kids as the end goal and idolized it? How has our culture?
2. Who do you look to as a role model? What do you admire about them?
3. What things have you done in the past few years that you wouldn't have if you were married with kids?
4. If you don't get married, what else might God have you do with the next ten or twenty years of your life?

SIXTEEN

* * * * * *

How Can I Be Content, Thankful, and Joyful?

The man who has God for his treasure has all things in One. Many ordinary treasures may be denied him, or if he is allowed to have them, the enjoyment of them will be so tempered that they will never be necessary to his happiness. Or if he must see them go, one after one, he will scarcely feel a sense of loss, for having the Source of all things he has in One all satisfaction, all pleasure, all delight. Whatever he may lose he has actually lost nothing, for he now has it all in One, and he has it purely, legitimately and forever.

A. W. Tozer

Joy, contentment, and thankfulness can be elusive. A few rare people seem to naturally ooze these three things. I am not one of those people. I need to cultivate them. They do not automatically thrive in my heart.

Many days rather than seeking to cultivate these things, my focus is on what is lacking in my life. All I tend to see are the ways I am in need, in hunger, and in want. My thoughts tend to readily drift towards my lack of a husband. If my focus is on singleness, then my heart slides into sorrow, discontentment, and ingratitude. These sentiments seem to fill my heart more often than I want to admit.

Discontentment comes when my desires for the gifts of God in this life trump my desire for God Himself. I want to be content with whatever He has for me now. I want to be at peace with what I have, not only longing for something different or new. Paul said it is possible to learn to be content when in need, in hunger, or in want (Phil. 4:11–12).

For me, the key to joy, contentment, and thankfulness is to remember who God is and what He has already done for me. It is also important for me to intentionally recognize all that is good in my day-to-day life.

I have found the more I cultivate thankfulness in my life, the easier it is to feel joyful and content. Days are still hard, but they are easier to bear when viewed through the lens of gratitude.

COUNT THE LITTLE BLESSINGS

There are many things to be thankful for if only I would recognize them. When my focus is on what I do not have, I tend to overlook the good things in my life. In Luke 17, Jesus heals ten lepers. Only one out of the ten men returns to thank Jesus. It would probably be generous to say I thank Jesus for one out of every ten blessings in my life.

Compared to previous generations, we have an excess of material blessings. Most of us do not need any more clothes or shoes. We may want new clothes and shoes, but most of us already have more than enough. Do we thank the Lord for what we have, or are we caught up in the pursuit for more?

In the back of my journals, I have started compiling lists

of good moments and little blessings. The blessings I appreciate the most in this life tend to be good moments: a sweet conversation with a friend, a group of friends laughing, and a beautiful day I get to enjoy. Pausing to appreciate the goodness of these moments helps me cultivate a deeper sense of gratitude. We should "give thanks in all circumstances" (1 Thess. 5:18). This verse is often quoted but rarely obeyed. Most of the time, we fail to give thanks in good circumstances, let alone when things are hard.

It is also good to develop the ability to go through the worst circumstances and in those moments find things to be thankful for. The more difficult the situations, the more aggressive I am at looking for those things.

Even in traumatic circumstances, it is important to find specific things to be thankful for. It helps me to see the grace of God in those moments. I want to see things to be thankful for in burglaries, in hospitals, and in nightmares. I also want to be grateful when I am in want, in hunger, and in need. For me, thankfulness is the path to contentment. If I want to be content with my circumstances, I first need to be thankful in them.

Gospel-Centered Gratitude

Learning to give thanks in all circumstances is good, but the source of my gratitude needs to be something more permanent than ever-changing circumstances. On the whole, I do not want the majority of my thankfulness to flow out of what is temporary. I want it to be rooted in the unshakable truth of what the Lord has already done for me. We are prone to forget. We fail to remember. If we do not remind ourselves of what the Lord has done for us, the world certainly will not remind us.

"Remember that . . . you were separate . . . excluded . . . foreigners . . . without hope . . . without God . . . you who once were far away have been brought near by the blood of Christ" (Eph. 2:12, 13). There is much we need to remember. Think about the weight and implications of each of these words: separated, excluded, foreigners, without hope . . . *without God.* An abiding satisfaction comes when we realize what it means to have God. If we have Him, we have everything we need; He is enough. Husbands and babies are great, but God is better. He came for you. He brought you near to Him. Remember that truth! Be thankful and rejoice for all you have in Him.

Even when the circumstances of my life seem to be upside down and nothing seems to be turning out the way I wanted, I want to be thankful for what He did for me on the cross. The best and greatest thing God will ever or could ever do for us is to bring us near and into His presence. If we think God needs to do something else in order for us to be thankful, we do not understand what He has already done.

When it comes to remembering who the Lord is and what He has done for us, we could make a long list. I have found it helpful to have a short list of three things. Three things I can quickly turn to and meditate on. It is great to make a long list, and I would encourage you to make one. However, if you train your mind to remember three specific things, they will be there in even the darkest moments.

I learned this last year when I did an extended forty-days of prayer. I had specific things I was praying over, but I wanted to start each time by praising and thanking the Lord. I picked three things to thank the Lord for every time I prayed. I would spend five to fifteen minutes thanking God for these three things: His unfailing love, His mercy, and His forgiveness. What I specifically said was different each time, but it was always about these three things.

Now in difficult situations when I pray, these things automatically come to my mind. Going over these truths, again and again, helped me cultivate a deeper appreciation for them. Since dwelling on these three areas has encouraged my heart, I want to expand a bit on each one.

LOVE, MERCY, AND FORGIVENESS

When we are at a loss for what we can be thankful for, we can always be thankful for the unfailing love of God. "O God, we meditate on your unfailing love" (Ps. 48:9). We can never meditate on God's love too much. The devil loves it when we doubt the God's love or think His love has failed. We need to regularly stop and reflect on the Lord's unfailing love.

He did not have to reveal his love to us. He could have left us here wondering if He is a God who loves messed up people like us, but He did not do that. We do not have to sit here extrapolating our circumstances, trying to determine if God loves us. He has revealed His love to us, and He has clearly demonstrated it.

It is a thousand times more likely that we will fail to love God than God will fail to love us. Actually, it is probably closer to a trillion. We have likely already failed to love God a thousand different times, but He can never fail to love us. His love is constant. Human love is fickle, but God's love never changes. Whether single, married, divorced, or widowed, His unfailing love is sufficient.

As I have grown in my knowledge of who God is, the

more I grasp the disparity between Him and me. If the Lord was not merciful, who could stand? I fall short in a thousand ways. My selfishness, my pride, my frustration, and my concern for the opinion of others are always getting in the way. They are also always reminding me of my need for mercy.

One of my favorite songs has a line that really resonates with me. "Oh Lord You know the hearts of men and still You let them live."[1] When I read the accounts in the Bible of the Lord striking people dead, I stand in awe. Not because God did such a thing, but because I have not suffered the same fate. The human heart is desperately wicked (Jer. 17:9 NLT), but I do not need the Bible to tell me that. I see it in my own heart, and I see it in the world.

Throughout the Bible, it describes God as merciful. A couple of years ago, a verse stuck out to me that says, "God delights to show mercy" (Mic. 7:18). Thankfully, I have a God who delights in showing mercy because I am in desperate need of it. I am also challenged because I should "love mercy" (Mic. 6:8) and "be merciful, just as your Father is merciful" (Luke 6:36). God delights in showing mercy; do I delight in showing mercy as well? The more I grasp the depth of mercy that God has shown me, the more I will show it to others. When people are cruel, rude, or irritating—how do you respond?

God can always show me mercy because all my sin was dealt with on the cross. Jesus died for all of it. "He forgave us all our sins, having canceled the charge of our legal indebtedness, which stood against us and condemned us; he has taken it away, nailing it to the cross" (Col. 2:13–14). I can forever and always be thankful that God made a way for my sins to be forgiven.

When life feels unfair, it is good to remember what I deserve if my sins count against me. I deserve punishment and hell. It is when I lose sight of this that I become disgruntled and dissatisfied with what God has given me. When I think of what I deserve, I am overwhelmed with gratitude.

I want a deep appreciation for the forgiveness of God to mark my life. In Christ, I have so many blessings that endure regardless of my temporary situation. They are an overflow of having my sins forgiven through faith in Him. Instead of focusing on what else I want, I am trying to cultivate a heart of thankfulness for what God has already given me.

After my forty days of prayer ended, I continued to wake up in the morning and thank God for His unfailing love, mercy, and forgiveness. Regardless of what this life holds or does not hold, I want to praise Him. He has blessed me so much, and I do not want to be ungrateful. He has revealed His heart to us, so we do not need to doubt it.

> Has his unfailing love vanished forever?
> Has his promise failed for all time?
> Has God forgotten to be merciful?
> Has he in anger withheld his compassion?
> (Ps. 77:8–9)

We have the incredible blessing of being able to answer all these questions with a resounding, "No." Forever and always we have the ability to simply look to the cross when we question God's heart toward us. We should not need anything other than an understanding of what happened on the cross to be joyful.

His love will never vanish, but it remains forever. His

promises never fail. He does not forget to be merciful, but His mercy is new every morning (Lam. 3:23). Time and time again He has demonstrated His compassion to us. As I grasp the reality of this, joy floods my heart.

Reading this section will likely change very little in your heart. Spending time in prayer praising God for these things will. Every day for the next three weeks, spend at least five minutes thanking God and see how it impacts your heart. If you were to pick three things that you can always be thankful for, what would you pick? The best weapon against bitterness is thankfulness.

A HEART OF JOY

Even after all of that, I question whether I am joyful and excited enough about what the Lord has done for me. In the break room at my job, we have big screen TVs. It is common to find a game show on when you walk into the room. Last year, every time I saw a game show I noticed the same thing.

People get so excited when their name is called. Doors open to reveal the prize they have a chance to win, and they go crazy with excitement. They jump up and down. They are screaming at the top of their lungs.

I am sitting there thinking, "You do realize you have not won anything yet?" Seriously, if people have a chance to win a car, they lose their minds. Most of the time they do not end up winning it.

As I reflect on their responses, I am convicted. Am I as excited, joyful, and thankful for what God has done for me as the people on the TV game shows? I am not really the "scream and jump up and down" type. Occasionally, I think of how excited, joyful, thankful I would be if the man I liked asked me out. I would be more likely to burst into tears than scream, but internally I would be rejoicing. What the Lord has already done for me is incomparably better than winning a car or this man asking me out.

Game shows demonstrate how people respond when they win even little prizes. People's enthusiasm for things that will not matter ten years from now convicts me of my lack of thankfulness for what will matter for all eternity.

I need to cultivate a heart of joy. One of my pastors regularly speaks about the passage where Jesus's disciples come back from the mission work Jesus sent them to do and they are excited to talk about what they have done. Jesus says to them, "However, do not rejoice that the spirits submit to you, but rejoice that your names are written in heaven" (Luke 10:20). You should not just rejoice in ministry success because you will not always have success in ministry.

The disciples had done well and been successful. Jesus's instruction was not a consolation prize. It was not that they had failed, and He was encouraging them to rejoice anyway. They had done well, and Jesus tells them not to rejoice in it, but to rejoice in heaven. Our deepest sense of joy needs to overflow out of the prospect of heaven.

There is joy in seeing someone you have spent time with making choices to follow Jesus, and it is disheartening to see them walk away from the Lord. If you care about people, that will be true. However, all of our joy should not be wrapped up in others. We should have a deep sense of abiding joy in the Lord.

My pastor says he regularly prays, "Lord help me to be content just in serving You." Regardless of whether we see a lot of fruit and success in ministry, we should simply be content in serving the Lord.

I have tweaked this for my life. I pray, "Lord, help me to be content just serving You in singleness." Whatever my situation in life, I want a heart that is content with simply serving the Lord. If I am going to be single the rest of my life, I do not want a disgruntled heart to hold me back from living for Him and being a light to others.

Life is short and there are so many ways we can spend our days. I want to spend mine loving and serving the Lord. Some aspects of my life may not turn out the way I want them to turn out. The more my focus is on setting up my life here the way I want it, the more my joy depends upon seeing it happen.

When I am discouraged I need to evaluate what I am focusing on. I need to shift my focus to what I am thankful for right now. The less thankful I am, the more discontent I am. The more discontent I am, the less I want to be thankful. It is a downward spiral, but the opposite is also true. The more intentional I am about being thankful, the more natural the response becomes. Try it three times a day for twenty-one days; you will see what I mean.

To me, joy, contentment, and thankfulness seem to be the three strands of a cord. All three can be found in dwelling on what the Lord has done for us. Our joy should always be rooted in the cross and the hope of heaven. True contentment is found in walking with God and serving Him. Even if our dreams for this life do not come true, we always have reasons to rejoice. The world needs single women who will point to Jesus as the source of joy and contentment.

JOURNAL QUESTIONS

1. Paul said, "I have learned to be content" (Phil. 4:11). Do you think of contentment as something you can learn? Why or why not?

2. How do you see joy, contentment, and thankfulness intertwined in your heart?

3. When can you build into your regular schedule time to intentionally reflect on what you are thankful for?

4. List ten reasons why you are thankful that you are single today.

5. What are your two biggest takeaways from this book?

Appendix – My Story

Like most eighteen-year-olds, I came to college thinking I had life pretty much figured out. It didn't take me long to realize that this wasn't true. When it came to God, Jesus, heaven, and hell, I had a lot of misconceptions.

I started going to a small group Bible study that met in my dorm, and I felt like everyone knew way more than I did. After a few weeks, I began regularly having dinner with one of the upperclassman girls. During one of the meals, she told me about when she became a Christian. She talked about realizing she deserved to go to hell. She said she was so thankful that Jesus died on the cross for her.

In that moment, I stopped listening to what she was saying. My mind started racing.

Surely, she didn't mean what she just said. It can't be true, but it must be. She knows so much more than I do. How can it be true? My dear friend is the nicest, sweetest, kindest person I've ever met. She really loves Jesus. She reads her Bible every day. She gets up early to pray.

If there is anyone I've ever met that deserves to go to heaven, it is her. What's the worst she's ever done? Been mean to her sisters when she was five? Told a lie? Disobeyed her parents? I know her. I know she has never done anything much worse than these little sins. If these are the worst things she's ever done, how can she look me in the eye and tell me she deserves to go to hell?

If she deserves to go to hell, then certainly there is no

hope for me. I deserve the same thing. I've never considered that before.

If lying disqualifies a person from deserving to go to heaven, then long ago I was disqualified. High school was a season of lying for me. If my lips were moving, I was probably lying or giving some half-truth. I developed a habit of telling people whatever they wanted to hear, regardless of whether it was true. Lies often made people happier than the truth.

Growing up I thought, good people go to heaven, and really bad people go to hell. I had always thought that as long as I did more good than bad, I was good to go.

Learning that this wasn't the case wasn't what I expected to learn at college. Hearing that any and all sin separates me from God wasn't what I wanted to hear. I knew that God is perfect and holy, but I had never pictured standing before Him trying to tell Him that I deserved to go to heaven.

I had always tried to be self-sufficient, and it's hard for self-sufficient people to admit they need help. However, I realized that there was no way that with all my sin I could stand before a perfect and holy God and tell him I deserved to go to heaven. Unfortunately, there was more; not only did I not deserve to go to heaven, but my sin deserved to be punished.

God is a perfect judge, and He can't leave sin unpunished. Recognizing I deserved to be punished for my sin was tough to swallow. There was sin in my life, I knew that, but my biggest issue was pride. I thought I was good enough to deserve to go to heaven. I was drowning in pride. My pride kept me from seeing my need for a Savior.

I realized God sees everything in my life: all the anger,

all the hatred, all the lies, all the lust, all the selfishness, all the pride. Before God, we are all completely exposed.

It was only when I understood that I had no hope of being good enough to go to heaven that I began to understand why Jesus died on the cross. If we could be good enough, Jesus didn't need to die.

The punishment that I deserve for my sins was placed on Him. Everything that disqualifies me from a relationship with God and from going to heaven was dealt with on the cross. When I was eighteen, I realized my need for a Savior.

Up until that point in my life, my faith and trust had been in myself. I had faith that I was good enough to deserve to go to heaven and trusted that the good things I had done would get me in. Now my faith is in Jesus, that He died for my sins, and I trust that because of what He has done for me I will go to heaven when I die. I want to follow and serve Him not in order to earn my way to heaven but because I am thankful for all that He has done for me.

Sin in our lives after we become a Christian can be confusing for people. Yes, we should repent and turn from our sin when we become a Christian. Sin shouldn't be a secret pet we continue feeding. Sometimes we need to address underlying causes and contributing factors in order to uproot sin from our lives. Ultimately, even the best Christians still sin. No matter how much a Christian grows spiritually, they will never out grow their need of Savior. At the end of the day, we are all human beings desperately in need of Jesus. In my life, this is as true today as it was the day I first became a Christian.

When I became a Christian, I started to read my Bible every day. I had a lot of misconceptions about the Bible, and

I wanted to know what was actually written in it. It helped me to learn who God really is and what it means to follow Him. We will never outgrow our need to have the Word of God in our lives daily. There is no equivalent substitute for it. If you have never read the entire Bible, I encourage you to add it your bucket list. Not as something you'll start in the future, but as something you will start today. There are many different English translations. Be sure you have a translation you easily understand. If you want to see the differences look up John 3 in different versions. If you've never read the Bible, the book of John is a great place to start.

If you have never placed your faith and trust in Jesus Christ for your salvation, won't you consider doing it right now? You can pray to God now, and He will hear you. What do you pray? There are no special words. Simply verbally: Recognize your sin. Repent of your sin. Repent of your pride (thinking you could be good enough to deserve heaven on your own). Ask God to forgive you for all your sins. Believe that Jesus died to pay for your sin. Place your faith and trust in Jesus's death and resurrection as the reason why you believe you will go to heaven when you die. Ask God to help you live in a way that honors what Jesus has done for you. Take time to pray now. (If you prayed and you know someone who is a Christian, tell them about it.)

For those of you who thought the "My Story" section was going to be my story of dating, relationships, and singleness, I'm sorry I disappointed you. I have no story to share. I dated three guys in high school, became a Christian my first semester in college, and haven't had a serious relationship since. I have been single for twelve years and counting.

I have to go through the truths of this book on a regular

basis. My own heart is not immune to discouragement or dis-contentment. I want to cling to what is true and press on to finish this race well. Jesus gave His life in exchange for mine, may I always be willing to give up my dreams in exchange for His.

ACKNOWLEDGMENTS

Who am I that the Lord has brought me this far? It is humbling to think of where I was ten years ago. The Lord has refined my heart so much in the past decade. If any truth in this book encourages your heart, it is by the grace of God.

While writing this book I have often thought: this is crazy, stupid, and impossible. I almost quit a hundred times. Whenever I was ready to give up someone would encourage me in some little way.

I have a degree in Biochemistry and Molecular Biology, not English. When it comes to writing, I need all the help I can get. First, I need to thank Lauren. She proofread the rough draft of this book, graciously pointing out my novice errors. I also want to thank Laura who helped refine and polish the final version.

There is a huge thanks owed to my friends, sisters, and pastors' wives who read random chapters of this book. Their feedback helped hone the content of each chapter.

The cover, my photo, and my website were all done by my wonderful friend Bekah.

I also want to thank Hannah, who has heard more of my angst about singleness than the rest of my friends combined. She always encourages me to remember what is true, and she directs my heart back to the Lord.

I hope this book has encouraged you, challenged you, and made you laugh. If you would take a moment to write a review for the book on Amazon, it will help others find it. More than anything, I hope this book prompts conversation between you and the women in your life.

NOTES

Chapter 5
[1] C. S. Lewis, *The Silver Chair* (New York, NY: Scholastic Inc., 1995), 27. Extract reprinted by permission.

Chapter 6
[1] Joy Whitney, *With a Whole Heart*, 4th ed. (Great Commission Northwest, 2006), 61–62.

Chapter 7
[1] Rabbi Meir Ben Isaac, *Akdamut* (Worms, Germany: 1050). This modification was found written on the wall of an insane asylum and were used as lyrics in a song by Frederick Lehman.

Chapter 10
[1] Amy Carmichael, "Make Pure," in *Rose from Brier* (The Dohnavur Fellowship, 1933). Used by permission of CLC Publications. May not be further reproduced. All rights reserved.
[2] C. S. Lewis, *The Great Divorce* (New York, NY: Harper-Collins, 2001), 75. Extract reprinted by permission.

Chapter 11

[1] Susanna Wesley, in a letter, June 8, 1725.

[2] In the Old Testament era, Samaria was a center of idol worship (1 Kings 16). Even in the New Testament era, traditional Jews did not associate with Samaritans (John 4:9). In that culture, it was odd that Jesus went to Samaria, odd that He talked to a Samaritan, and even odder that He spoke to a woman alone.

[3] *While You Were Sleeping*, directed by Jon Turteltaub (1995; Burbank, CA: Hollywood Home Video, 1998), DVD.

[4] Here are some good resources you may find helpful:

    a. Books:
  - i. *Healing the Wounds of Sexual Addiction* by Mark Laaser
  - ii. *Taking Every Thought Captive* by Mark Laaser
  - iii. *Dirty Girls Come Clean* by Crystal Renaud
  - iv. *Beggar's Daughter* by Jessica Harris
  - v. *Swipe Right* by Levi Lusko
  - vi. *The Game Plan* by Joe Dallas

    b. Video (YouTube)
  - i. Jeromy Darling "Love&Sex&Porn"

    c. Websites (filtering)
  - i. covenanteyes.com
  - ii. netnanny.com
  - iii. qustodio.com
  - iv. meetcircle.com
  - v. usa.kaspersky.com
  - vi. mobicip.com

    d. Websites (other resources)
  - i. faithfulandtrue.com
  - ii. joedallas.com
  - iii. dirtygirlsministries.com

Chapter 12
[1] Elisabeth Elliot, in *The Elisabeth Elliot Newsletter*, accessed June 10, 2017,
http://www.elisabethelliot.org/newsletters/july-aug-94.pdf.
[2] Corrie ten Boom, *The Hiding Place*, 35th Anniversary ed. (Grand Rapids, MI: Chosen Books, 2006), 188.

Chapter 15
[1] Corrie ten Boom, *The Hiding Place*, 35th Anniversary ed. (Grand Rapids, MI: Chosen Books, 2006), 118–20, 144–48, 45–61.
[2] Corrie ten Boom, *Tramp for the Lord* (Grand Rapids, MI: Revell, 1974).
[3] Elisabeth Elliot, *Passion and Purity* (Old Tappan, NJ: Revell, 1984), 168, 13.
[4] Elisabeth Elliot, *The Savage My Kinsman*, rev. ed. (Ann Arbor, MI: Servant Books, 1981), 60.
[5] Elisabeth Elliot, "About Elisabeth," accessed July 12, 2017, http://elisabethelliot.org/about.html.
[6] Elisabeth Elliot, *A Chance to Die* (Old Tappan, NJ: Revell, 1987), 133, 372, 173–79, 146.
[7] Rosemary Kingsland, *A Saint Among Savages* (St James's Place, London: Collins, 1980), 24, 13, 114–15, 122.
[8] Janet & Geoff Benge, *Rachel Saint: A Star in the Jungle* (Seattle, WA: Youth With A Mission, 2005), 168–70, 205.
[9] Miriam Huffman Rockness, *A Passion for the Impossible* (Grand Rapids, MI: Discovery House, 2003), 83–85, 98, 327.
[10] ten Boom, *The Hiding Place*, 69–71, 96, 173.
[11] Elliot, *A Chance to Die*, 41–43.
[12] Kingsland, *A Saint Among Savages*, 34.
[13] Rockness, *A Passion for the Impossible*, 89–91.
[14] Elisabeth Elliot, *These Strange Ashes* (San Francisco: Harper & Row, 1975), 42–45.

Chapter 16

Made in the USA
San Bernardino, CA
19 August 2018